Life in Colonial America

The Military in Colonial America

Carol Ellis

Cavendish Square
New York

Published in 2015 by Cavendish Square Publishing, LLC
243 5th Avenue, Suite 136, New York, NY 10016

First Edition

CPSIA Compliance Information: Batch # WS14CSQ

All websites were available and accurate when this book was sent to press.

Library of Congress Cataloging-in-Publication Data

Ellis, Carol.
The military in colonial America / by Carol Ellis.
p. cm. — (Life in colonial America)
Includes index.
ISBN 978-1-62712-897-1 (hardcover) ISBN 978-1-62712-899-5 (ebook)
1. United States — History — Colonial period, ca. 1600 - 1775. 2. United States — Militia. 3. United States. Continental Army — History. 4. United States — History — Revolution, 1775-1783. I. Ellis, Carol, 1945-. II. Title.
E188 .E57 2015
973.2—d23

Editorial Director: Dean Miller
Editor: Fletcher Doyle
Senior Copy Editor: Wendy A. Reynolds
Art Director: Jeffrey Talbot
Designer: Joseph Macri
Production Editor: David McNamara
Production Manager: Jennifer Ryder-Talbot

The photographs in this book are used by permission through the courtesy of: Cover photo by Dennis K. Johnson/Lonely Planet Images/Getty Images; Library of Congress Prints and Photographs Division/The surrender of Cornwallis at Yorktown A.D. 1781, 4; Andrews, John/File:A new map of the British colonies in North America(...) (2674323015).jpg/Wikimedia Commons, 5; Susan Isakson/Alamy, 6; North Wind/North Wind Picture Archives, 11; Hulton Archive/Getty Images, 13; Walker Art Library/Alamy, 14; North Wind/North Wind Picture Archives, 16; Interim Archives/Archive Photos/Getty Images, 19; North Wind/North Wind Picture Archives, 20; Stock Montage/Archive Photos/Getty Images, 23; North Wind/North Wind Picture Archives, 24; MPI/Archive Photos/Getty Images, 26–27; North Wind/North Wind Picture Archives, 28; North Wind/North Wind Picture Archives, 30; North Wind/North Wind Picture Archives, 32; North Wind/North Wind Picture Archives, 33; Newagen Archive/The Image Works, 35; Engrav'd Printed & Sold by Paul Revere Boston. The print was copied by Revere from a design by Henry Pelham for an engraving eventually published under the title "The Fruits of Arbitrary Power, or the Bloody Massacre," of which only two impressions could be located by Brigham. Revere's print appeared on or about March 28, 1770./File:Boston Massacre high-res.jpg/Wikimedia Commons, 38; Unknown, 19th century/File: Pontiac in 1763.jpg/Wikimedia Commons, 40; North Wind/North Wind Picture Archives, 42; Niday Picture Library/Alamy, 44; Cockpit Hill Factory, Derby, England. User:Calliopejen1 took the photo/File:Stamp Act Repeal'd.jpg/Wikimedia Commons, 45; North Wind/North Wind Picture Archives, 47; Universal Images Group/Getty Images, 48; English School/ The Bridgeman Art Library/Getty Images, 50; Time & Life Pictures/Getty Images, 51; Pictorial Press Ltd/Alamy, 53; MPI/Archive Photos/Getty Images, 55; Domenick D'Andrea/File:BattleofLongisland.jpg/Wikimedia Commons, 57; Bridgeman Art Library/Getty Images, 58; CHM\UIG, 59; Library of Congress Prints and Photographs Division/Washington at Valley Forge, 60; Christopher Mir/File: Major General Friedrich Wilhelm Augustus Baron von Steuben by Ralph Earl.jpeg/Wikimedia Commons, 62; John Trumbull/File: Surrender of Lord Cornwallis.jpg/Wikimedia Commons, 67.

Printed in the United States of America

Contents

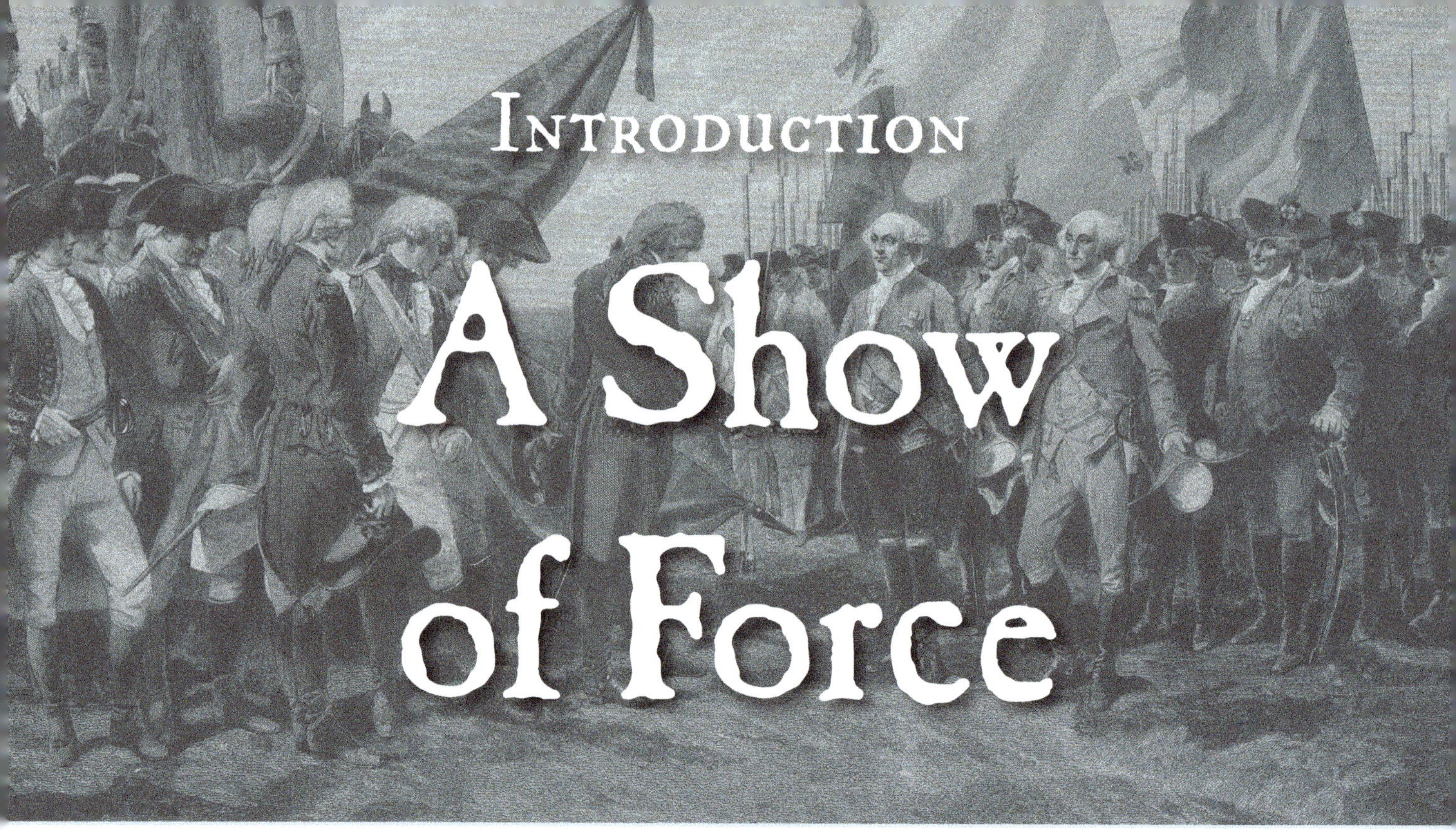

Introduction

A Show of Force

On October 19, 1781, after more than six years of war, the British army surrendered to the American colonial forces at Yorktown, Virginia. There would be a few more **skirmishes**, but the Revolutionary War was all but over.

The story goes that as the British troops surrendered, their band played the song "The World Turned Upside Down."

If ponies rode men and grass ate cows,
And cats were chased into holes by the mouse . . .
If summer were spring and the other way round,
Then all the world would be upside down.

The world had definitely turned upside down for the British. After all, England was, at the time, one of the most powerful nations in the world. The thirteen American colonies weren't yet a unified nation, and they were still struggling to survive in the New World. The British had hundreds of years of military experience and leaders who had organized troops for participation in many battles. The Continental Army, however, was only six years old.

But the Continental Army had help from France and Spain—and it had George Washington, who was able to take the colonial troops and lead them to victory. Who were these colonial troops? How were they trained? What wars had they fought? What weapons and tactics did they use? How did it all get started? The answers are as different as the colonies themselves.

At the beginning of the Revolutionary War, the thirteen colonies were in the hands of the British. Most of the early settlers, beginning with those in Jamestown, Virginia, in 1607, had come from England. But others had come from Germany, the Netherlands, Scotland, and Ireland. They came for different reasons: religious and political freedoms, and to make money. The areas of land they settled were different as well, so some became farmers while others became ironworkers. But one thing they all had in common was the need for protection. France and Spain had already established themselves in other parts of North America, and British colonists were wary that they might try to force them out. But their first concern was protecting themselves from Native Americans, whose homeland they had invaded.

The Military in Colonial America will explore ways that the colonists protected themselves, the battles they fought and who fought them, and how they adapted their military to fit the "New World."

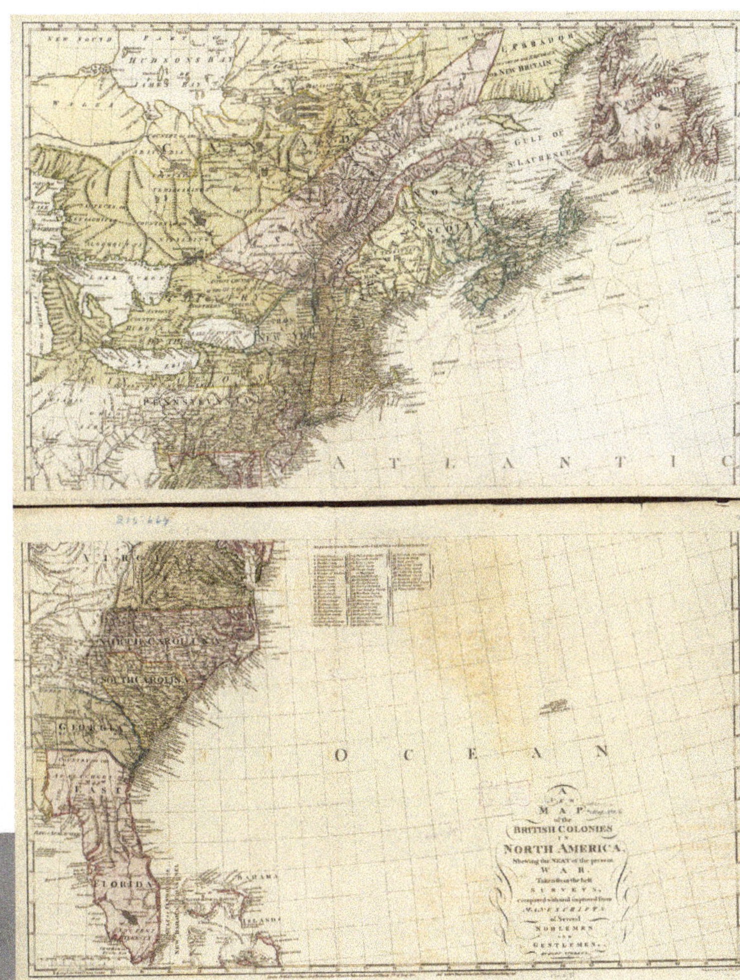

British colonies in North America hugged the eastern coastline, from what would become the state of Georgia in the south, up to Massachusetts in the north.

Chapter One

Need for Defense

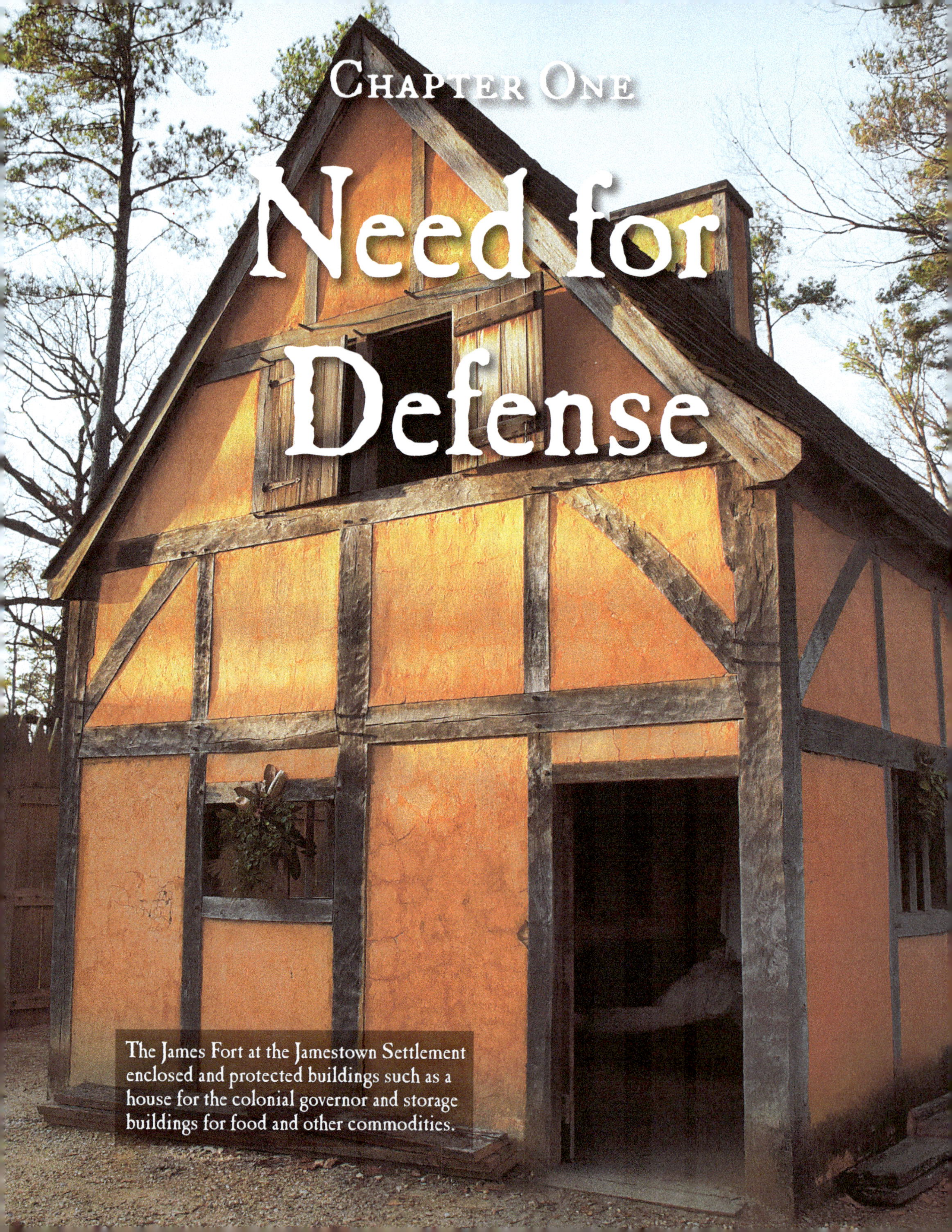

The James Fort at the Jamestown Settlement enclosed and protected buildings such as a house for the colonial governor and storage buildings for food and other commodities.

"The fifteenth of June, we had built and finished our Fort, which was triangle wise: having three Bulwarkes [one] at every corner, like a halfe Moone, and four or five pieces of Artillerie mounted in them."
—Jamestown settler James Percy on James Fort

The first English settlers arrived in what would become the state of Virginia in May 1607. By June, they had built James Fort, which burned down in January 1608 and apparently was immediately replaced. By 1619, a Virginia statute required everyone to attend church on the **Sabbath** "both forenoon and afternoon and all such as bear arms shall bring their pieces, swords, powder and shot."

Many of the Pilgrims who came to North America for religious freedom were **Puritans**. They also came with Myles Standish, a military advisor. Captain Standish organized the construction of a fort at Plymouth, and made sure there were cannons atop the first church the Puritans built.

Lord Baltimore, the founder of Maryland, published a list of arms and equipment that each man arriving in his colony was required to have. The list included a musket, a sword, ten pounds of gunpowder, and forty pounds of lead. Shortly after the Dutch colony of New Netherlands was taken over by England and renamed New York, the Duke of York gave orders for the arming of its people. "Besides the general stock of each town, every male within this government from sixteen to sixty years of age" with a few exceptions, had to be armed. Heads of households had to pay for the arms, including those for servants.

No one in the New World took safety for granted. Even though most of the settlers were British, they were on their own. When not at war, Britain reduced the size of its army, which was expensive to maintain, to a shell. During those times a standing army—a permanent army of professional soldiers—was not maintained. Even if it had had such an army, a request for help from the colonies could not be quickly answered. It would have taken soldiers weeks to sail across the Atlantic Ocean. The settlers then had to rely mostly on themselves for protection against Native Americans or rival European powers. But just having forts, cannons, and guns wasn't enough. The colonists needed people who were trained to fight effectively when they were called on. Their solution was the **militia** system.

Citizen Soldiers

"First, a law [is] to be made for the training of all the men in the country fit to bear arms, unto the exercise of military discipline . . ."

The militia system has a long history. As far back as the Middle Ages, laws required common people to purchase weapons and maintain them in their homes so they would be ready to protect their king and the state. England, during the seventh century, had developed a militia system requiring even the lowest class of **freemen** to maintain arms and be subject to a call for military duty. Its militia was the body of "citizens, burgesses, free tenants, villeins [serfs] and others from 15 to 60 years of age."

By the time the colonists arrived in the New World, many European countries relied less on the militia system and more on professional, paid armies. But the colonies couldn't afford professional armies. Even if they could have, most of the colonists would not have wanted to participate, as there was a deep distrust of the standing armies of the Old World. Those armies represented tyranny and the power of the throne. Many of the colonists had fled that power for religious and political reasons. Even though most of the settlers came from England, and the land was part of the British Empire, the colonies weren't yet a single, united country. Each colony had its own government and its own needs. And each one knew best how to organize its own militia.

Despite being organized by different colonies, the individual militias had a lot in common. For one, service was **compulsory** by law. There were, however, a few exceptions. Members of the clergy did not have to serve and some conscientious objectors would be excused. Slaves were almost always forbidden to serve because colonists, especially in the South, feared an armed uprising. Free blacks were allowed to serve in some of the colonies, but not in others. The colony of Pennsylvania was founded in 1681, and settled by Quakers, who were **pacifists**. They opposed all types of war because of their religious beliefs. Although voluntary militia groups formed, it wasn't until 1755 that the colony's government passed an act that established Pennsylvania's first group of paid, enlisted troops.

Society of Friends

The Society of Friends, or Quakers, was a religious group established in England in the 1600s. They were persecuted for, among other things, refusing to worship in the Church of England or to pay tithes to it, for not showing proper respect to their "superiors" (they believed that all men and women were equals), and for their opposition to war. They were among the first conscientious objectors, meaning people who, because of deeply held religious or moral beliefs, refuse to bear arms or serve in the military.

For white males in Colonial America—farmers, merchants, or fur traders between the ages of sixteen and sixty—joining the militia was usually a requirement. A certain number of musters, or training sessions, were mandatory to attend each year. Colonists with the means had to provide their own weapons. Most colonial governments kept a reserve supply and would furnish weapons to those who could not afford them. The governors of each colony usually appointed a militia's top commanders, but local officers were elected from a village or county.

Emergency Defenders

A member of the militia was expected to always be "on call" in case of an emergency. During the early years of the colonies, this usually meant an attack by Native Americans. Most were surprise attacks, and a militia company wouldn't have time to gather and fight as a group. Because of this, many settlements built **stockades** and **garrison** houses.

During an attack, settlers would head for safety in the garrison house. Militiamen would place a lookout in the highest points in the garrison. Native Americans would often loot the settlement and destroy the food supplies. The colonists, along with the militiamen, were usually able to wait out the attack. Although they often fired from within, they almost never went after the attackers. Once the raid was over, the colonists would return to their villages or farms to repair any damage.

The colonists never abandoned defense, but over time, they began using offensive measures to protect themselves. They organized military expeditions with the hope of defeating their attackers before they could strike. Most of the colonies also wanted to expand their frontiers and clear the way for more settlements.

For the military expeditions, the colonies began to use a voluntary militia. The numbers of men supplied by each colony were based on the colony's population. Because men held jobs and positions that kept the colonies working,

The clash of cultures between Native Americans and European colonists led to an escalation of violence, destruction, and death.

including tending crops and minding local businesses, areas or districts with fewer men could not operate or flourish in their absence. Thus smaller colonies supplied fewer men.

Men were offered bounties to volunteer, and many poor men joined for the money. Wealthier men often hired substitutes to take their places. If a colony or town couldn't supply enough male volunteers, it would initiate a draft system, whereby eligible males were ordered to serve. Unlike in today's draft system, the punishment for not serving was usually a fine. Whether they were rich or poor, volunteers or draftees, the militiamen signed up only for short periods. They insisted on the right to return to their homes and settlements, their farms or trades as soon as a battle or an expedition was over.

Colonial American Firearms

A militiaman in the early years of Colonial America most likely used a matchlock musket, which used a wick lit with a match to ignite the powder. A matchlock musket had a maximum range of 50 to 75 yards (46 to 69 meters) and its accuracy was limited. There were also the problems of loading it in the rain, or having the glow of a match disclose the militiamen's positions.

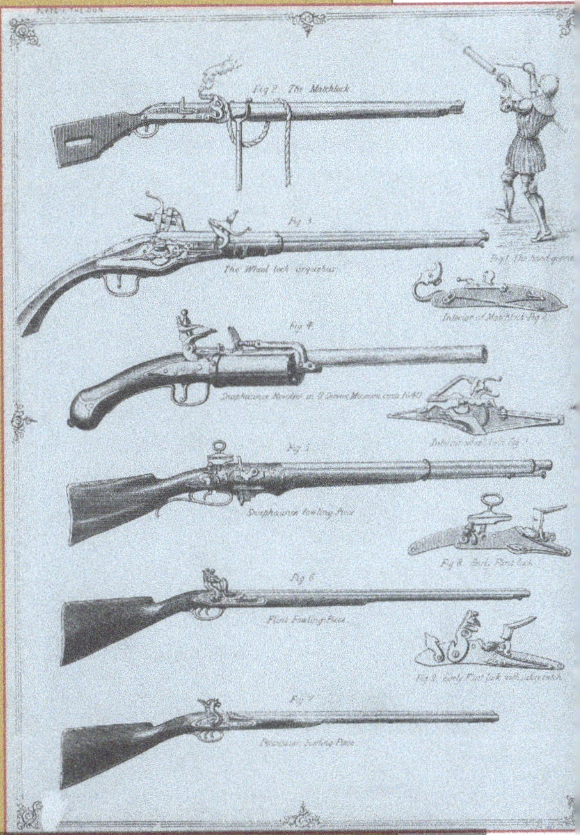

Guns had to be practical. Wood for the stocks had to resist warping, to promote accuracy. Scrolling on a brass trigger guard wasn't for show – it provided a better grip.

Around 1610, French court gunsmith Marin le Bourgeoys developed an improved firearm mechanism called the "flintlock." Flint and steel replaced the match light. When the trigger was pulled, the flint struck the steel and the spark this created ignited the powder. It was simpler, faster, and safer. It took several years for the flintlock to gain widespread use in the colonies. But by the 1630s and 1640s, it was used by most militia units.

In the early 1700s, Martin Mylin, a German immigrant to Lancaster County, Pennsylvania, perfected an improved version of the flintlock: the Pennsylvania long rifle. Its range was 200 to 300 yards. The rifle was so much more accurate that the colonists' marksmanship grew to become a valued and common skill.

Thanks to the range and accuracy of the long rifle, colonial marksmen began using their shooting skills to carry out "hit-and-run attacks" from longer distances, hiding behind the cover of trees and bushes in wilderness areas. The colonial militia would later use these tactics against the French during the French and Indian War and then during the Revolutionary War.

Chapter Two

Special Forces

Many of the early special forces were comprised of hunters, trappers, and woodsmen, men who could live off the land and use their knowledge of it to fight and stay alive.

"Tell the truth about what you see and what you do. There is an army depending on us for correct information. You can lie all you please when you tell other folks about the Rangers, but don't never lie to a Ranger or officer."

—Robert Rogers' Standing Orders for Army Rangers, No. 4

Colonial governments employed full-time soldiers called "rangers." The soldiers were named as such because they "ranged" through wooded areas and outskirts of settlements looking for signs of a Native American attack. Rangers served as somewhat of an early-warning system for the settlers, and were armed so they could quickly defend their settlement against hit-and-run tactics. In clashing with Native Americans, they learned and adapted new ways of fighting in the wilderness, techniques at which they soon became experts.

In time, Rangers began to take on a new role. In addition to patrolling and warning, they took the fight to the enemy by going deep into Native American territory. They would conduct raids and gather **intelligence**, or information, about what was happening and what might happen next.

Ranger companies began to form early in the colony settlements. They worked for the British because the colonies thought of themselves as part of the British Empire. One of the first Ranger units was led by Captain Benjamin Church of Massachusetts in 1676, during the war known as King Philip's War.

King Philip, or Metacom, was the leader of a group of Native American tribal allies in New England.

Church was an experienced fighter and woodsman. He'd learned how to fight in the wilderness by watching the defense techniques employed by Native Americans: hiding, striking from behind cover, blending into the forest. Church noted that Native Americans never moved together as a large group so there was never a great number of men to target. He instructed his rangers to move through the forests in the same way. He recommended that they wear **moccasins** so they'd walk quietly, and fight with hatchets so their gunfire wouldn't alert anyone to their presence.

The Rangers' skills became famous. In 1756, Robert Rogers was awarded command of an independent company, which began with sixty privates, two lieutenants, three sergeants, and an ensign.

Church also allied his troops with some Native Americans. Many of them opposed King Philip and were willing to fight with Church. In fact, his first company of rangers comprised about 200 paid volunteers, among which only about sixty were Englishmen. The remaining members were Native Americans. It was this ranging band that battled King Philip and a small group of his allies, an event that helped put an end to King Philip's War.

Gorham's Rangers were led first by Captain John Gorham and then by his brother, Joseph. The rangers were a mixed group of colonists and members of

Rules for Rangers

When the British asked Rogers to train some of their troops to use his tactics, he wrote "Rules for the Ranging Service": twenty-eight instructions on the techniques of "woods warfare" in North America, which included ambush, fight, pursue, and retreat. To many of the British and the colonists, it was a new way of fighting.

Rogers stated that rangers must "appear at roll-call every evening equipped each with a firelock, sixty rounds of powder and ball, and a hatchet." Each ranger's role should be clear, and all should be ready at a moment's notice.

When in the field, Rogers wrote, smaller scouting expeditions should march in single file and keep enough distance between them so that one shot wouldn't kill two men. If they were moving over soft ground, they should walk beside one another because it would make it harder for the enemy to track them. Even with large groups of rangers sent to conduct attacks, Rogers instructed that they divide into columns and march twenty yards apart. This would help prevent an entire group from being surrounded.

Rogers also gave directions on when to make camp: in darkness, on high ground if possible, with sentries assigned to keep watch. When it came to fighting, Rogers was practical. "Don't fire until the enemy is very close," he advised. That would cause surprise and confusion and offer a better chance of "rushing upon them with your hatchets and **cutlasses**"

Rogers' rules have since been updated and are still issued to the U.S. Army Rangers.

the Mohawk tribe of Native Americans. In the 1740s, Britain paid them to skirmish with Native American allies of the French. Later, they would become the force that helped capture the Fortress of Louisbourg in Nova Scotia, and guard British camps from the French and their Native American allies. In 1760, Gorham was promoted to major. His unit was then named "North American Rangers."

Rogers' Rangers was the most famous of the ranger companies. Organized and commanded by Robert Rogers, the unit began in the colony of New Hampshire in 1755 as part of a British regiment. The unit's job was to scout the area around Lake George, in New York. The rangers learned that the French were building a fort at Ticonderoga, where a huge battle would eventually take place.

Some of the British commanders admired the rangers' skill, endurance, and knowledge of the countryside. Rogers' Rangers became a big advantage for the British during the French and Indian War (1754–1763) as they scouted the land, conducted raids, and captured prisoners.

Like Benjamin Church, Robert Rogers taught his troops to use the Native American fighting techniques of camouflage and **stealth** to surprise opponents.

At a Moment's Notice

The minutemen—a group of men who fought on the side of the American colonies—became famous for the role they played at Lexington and Concord at the beginning of the Revolutionary War. But their history began more than a hundred years earlier.

In 1645, under the constant threat of Native American uprisings, the Massachusetts council ordered the commander of every militia company to appoint 30 percent of their soldiers "who shall be ready at half an hour's warning upon any service they shall be put by their chief military officers." These were the first minutemen. They were volunteers from the community—shopkeepers, blacksmiths, politicians, farmers, ministers, and teachers. Armed with their own muskets, powder, bullets, and bandolier (an over-the-shoulder wide belt with small pockets for cartridges) they came prepared to serve.

In the years leading up to the Revolutionary War, the colonies continued to strengthen their individual militias as well as their minutemen bands. In December 1774, the Massachusetts Provincial Congress instructed the towns to ensure that all minutemen be equipped with a "firearm, bayonet, pouch, knapsack, thirty rounds of cartridges and balls, and that they be trained three times a week, and oftener, as opportunity may offer." To encourage men to volunteer, the Provincial Congress recommended that the minutemen be paid for their services.

At the May 1775 Virginia convention, each district was instructed to raise and train a battalion of men to march at a minute's notice. The "Culpeper Minutemen" carried tomahawks and knives as well as their muskets and powder horns. They wore shirts that bore the words "Liberty or Death" in large white letters.

The minutemen—chosen for their loyalty, reliability, and physical strength—were all in their twenties. Leaders of the minutemen bands were older; many had fought in the French and Indian War. What made the minutemen different from traditional soldiers was their fighting style. Like the ranger companies, they used surprise and stealth as they hid behind walls and buildings to fire upon their enemies. They would soon employ these tactics when facing the British army.

Approximately seventy minutemen confronted the British as they marched into Lexington, Massachusetts on April 19, 1775. At the Concord Bridge, 300 to 400 armed colonists forced the British to retreat.

Chapter Three

Early Battles

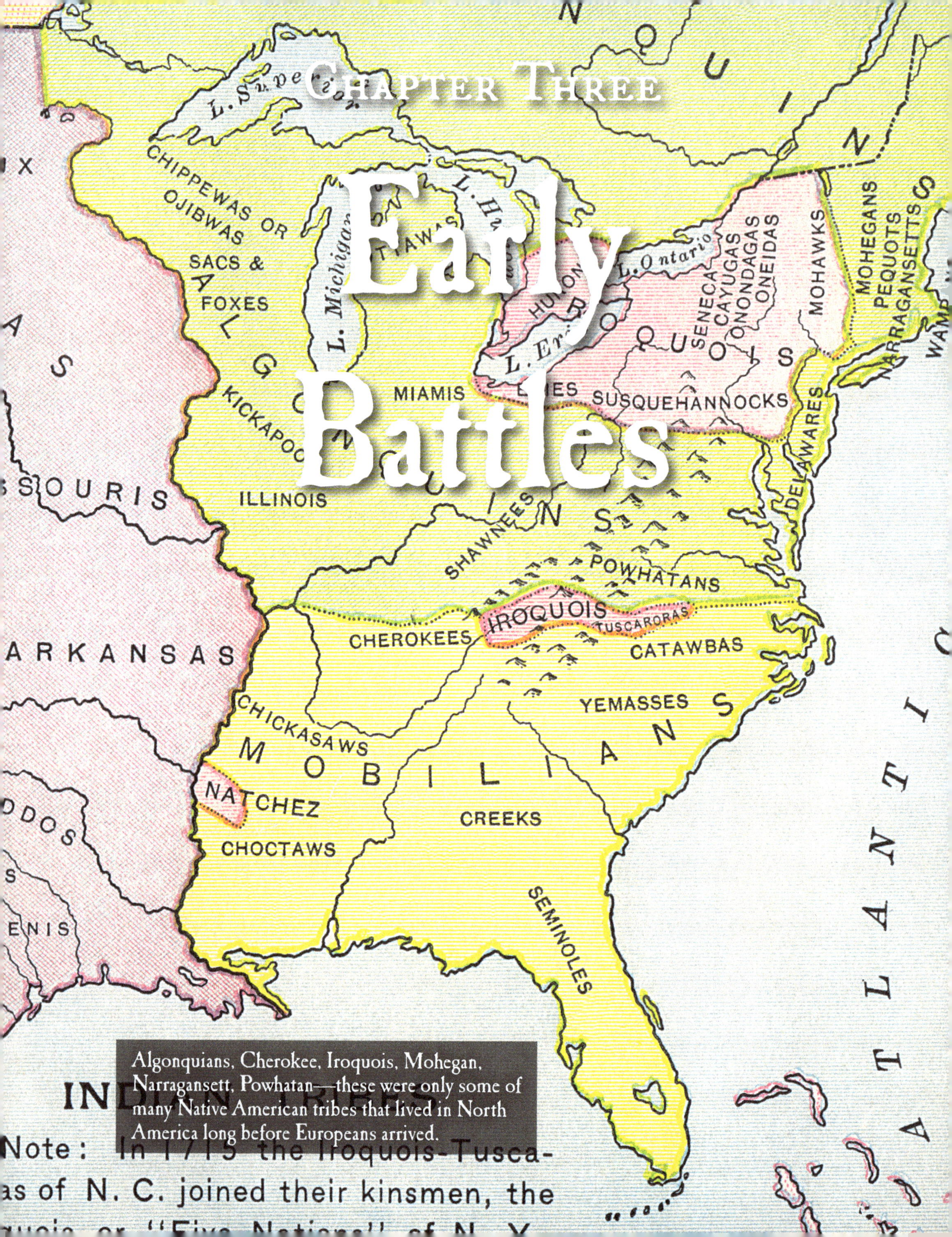

Algonquians, Cherokee, Iroquois, Mohegan, Narragansett, Powhatan—these were only some of many Native American tribes that lived in North America long before Europeans arrived.

> "... it is reported by themselves, that there were about foure hundred soules in this Fort, and not above five? of them escaped out of our hands."
>
> —Description of the Mystic Massacre by second in command John Underhill

When European colonists first landed in North America, they must have felt alone. During the very early years, many Native Americans, who had already lived there for centuries, were helpful to them. Powhatan, the chief of several Algonquian-speaking tribes, offered food to the newcomers in Virginia, trading it for weapons, blankets, and metal tools. The Wampanoag Indians in Massachusetts traded animal furs with the Pilgrims in exchange for wampum, or shell beads that were used as currency. They taught them what foods to gather and plant, and how to fish and hunt. In Connecticut, the Pequot traded furs—which were in great demand in Europe—for metal tools, cloth, and brass cookware.

But it wasn't long before conflict arose, especially over the land. The struggle for power grew fiercer over time, and the colonial military grew stronger.

The Tidewater Wars (1610–1646)

The Jamestown colony was established in 1607. By 1609, Powhatan's attitude toward the colonists had changed. He was certain they were going to "invade my people, possess my country." And Powhatan's vision soon came to pass.

When trade agreements sometimes went wrong, settlers became hostile, raiding Native American villages in the Tidewater area of Virginia for food. Colonists built more forts and practiced threatening military drills. They believed that Powhatan and his people should become Christians, and should think of themselves as subjects of the King of England.

Some members of Algonquian-speaking tribes went on the attack, burning crops and killing livestock. The colonists and the militia retaliated by taking hostages, and burning and destroying Native American villages.

Because tobacco had become a major source of income for the struggling colony, colonists wanted more land to expand the growth of this crop. Native Americans knew that this expansion would mean that more forests would be cleared, more game would be killed, and more **encroachment** into their areas would occur. They wanted the colonists out. In 1622, Powhatan's brother, Opechancanough, led a surprise raid on the settlements that left 25 percent of Virginia's colonists dead. The militia and the colonists struck back. This on-again, off-again battle raged for years. In 1644, Opechancanough led another large attack resulting in five hundred colonists being killed within the first day. But the colony's population had grown, and its military was stronger. In 1646, military forces captured and killed Opechancanough. The colonies eventually made treaties with the Native Americans, which gave the colonists rights to settle more and more land and confined the Powhatan people to smaller and smaller areas.

The Pequot War (1637)

Colonists pushed for more land and Native Americans tried to stop them from taking it. The colonial military then began to play a stronger role and thereby waged a stronger war. By the early 1630s, the English Puritan settlements at Plymouth, and the Massachusetts Bay Colonies, had started to expand. This took colonists into the Connecticut River Valley, and into battle with the Pequot Indians.

The Mystic Massacre caused most of the remaining Pequot to abandon their villages and territory, fearing more attacks by the British.

Even before colonists arrived in New England, Native Americans had competed and fought among themselves for control of the land and its resources. The conflicts caused weakness and instability in the region.

When the Europeans came, they brought diseases to which Native Americans had never been exposed. **Epidemics** of smallpox killed thousands. Even though their population had been cut almost in half because of fighting and disease, the Pequot remained powerful and in control. The Narragansett and the Mohegan tribes resented and feared the Pequot, and thus became allies of the British. The Pequot allied themselves with the Dutch, who at that time controlled much of what would become New York. The Dutch had also built trading posts in southeastern Connecticut. Both groups were in fierce competition not just for land, but also for the profits that could be made from the fur trade. Raids, skirmishes, and killings from both sides caused tensions to rise. In April 1637, a group of Pequot attacked English settlers on their way to the fields. They killed several men and women, and captured two young girls. Connecticut issued a declaration of war on the Pequot and joined forces with two other colonies—Plymouth and Massachusetts Bay—to face them in battle.

Declaration Of War

The first day of May, 1637...

It is ordered that there shall be an offensive war against the Pequot, and that there shall be ninety men levied out of the three plantations, Hartford, Wethersfield, and Windsor ... under the command of Captain John Mason.

Following the declaration of war, Captain John Mason of Windsor, commander of the Connecticut forces, mounted an expedition. His instructions were to attack the Pequot fortified villages at Mystic and Weinshauks.

When the colony of Connecticut declared war against the Pequot in 1637, it marked the first declared war in Connecticut between Native Americans and English colonists.

The major incident of the Pequot War, known as the Mystic Massacre, took place on May 26, 1637, before dawn. English troops from Connecticut and Massachusetts, their Native American allies, and militiamen surrounded a sleeping Pequot village and fort in Mystic, Connecticut. There were four hundred to seven hundred Pequot inside. Many of the men were away, so most in the village were women, children, and the elderly. The troops set the village afire. As the Pequot tried to escape, the soldiers followed instructions to either shoot or "destroy them by the sword." Hundreds of Pequot died during the attack. Only a handful escaped into the woods. Over the ensuing months, the military hunted down and captured many of the Pequot who hadn't been in Mystic that morning.

The Mystic Massacre signaled an end to the war. In September 1638, the English, the Narragansett, and the Mohegan signed the Treaty of Hartford.

Surviving Pequot were given to rival tribes or colonists as servants and slaves. Others were sold into slavery in Bermuda and the **West Indies**. Colonists declared the Pequot tribe extinct.

The Pequot war was the first time that Native Americans in New England had experienced such a "total war." The Native Americans—specifically those who were allies to the colonists—were appalled. This type of warfare, they argued, was "too furious, and slays too many men." The Native Americans became more wary than ever of the Europeans' fighting power. Many years would pass before another such war would break out.

King Philip's War (1675–1676)

Metacom (called King Philip by the colonists) was the leader of the Wampanoag Confederacy, which consisted of Native American tribes in New England. His father, Massasoit, had helped the Pilgrims of Plymouth survive their first harsh years in the land by teaching them how to grow their own crops. In 1621, Massasoit signed the Pilgrim-Wampanoag peace treaty with the settlers. Doing so sealed a promise of peace and mutual protection, and gave the Wampanoag the opportunity to trade for European goods, specifically firearms. The treaty also granted the newcomers the right to settle on 12,000 acres (4,856 hectare) of land.

The peaceful relationship lasted for many years, but by the time Philip became the tribal leader in 1662, things had changed. The population of the settlers had grown. By 1675, more and more settlements, towns, and villages had sprung up in Massachusetts, Rhode Island, and the Connecticut River Valley. The settlers wanted more land. Philip had sold some to them, but he resented the intrusion into Native American territories. He decided to stop selling land for seven years. The settlers decided to take what they wanted.

Convincing other tribes to join as allies, Philip became the leader of an open rebellion. King Philip's War began with an attack by a group of Wampanoag on the Massachusetts settlement of Swansea in June 1675. Leaders in Boston and Plymouth quickly responded by ordering a force to

burn the Wampanoag town at Mount Hope, Rhode Island. The conflict spread quickly. The colonies of Plymouth, Massachusetts, Connecticut, and Rhode Island, along with their own Native American allies and their militias, became involved.

In 1676, Captain Church and his troops hunted down Philip in his hiding place in Rhode Island. Philip was murdered—his severed head was put on display in Plymouth. Native Americans lost King Philip's War and their right to the land. From then on, colonists were free to expand their territory without interference.

King Philip's War between Native Americans and colonists lasted almost two years. One in ten soldiers on both sides were killed or wounded.

The New England colonists paid a price for winning the war. Hundreds of lives, homes, and villages were lost, and crops were destroyed. But a growing confidence in their military had been won. Despite the military's disorganization, its lack of well-trained militiamen, and little help from the British government— New England colonists won the war. Thus they believed that land was theirs.

Chapter Four

Global Wars Go Local

A series of global wars and conflicts would result in the expansion of British control in North America far beyond the eastern coastline.

"I heard the bullets whistle, and believe me, there is something charming in the sound."
—George Washington in a letter to his mother, May 3, 1754

By 1732, the thirteen colonies known as Colonial America were under control of the British. Those colonies were the areas where the British had first landed, settled, and established colonial governments. They'd taken New York from the Dutch and were pushing Native Americans farther from their lands. But compared to the entire North American continent, Colonial America was a small area.

Britain was not the first European power on the continent. Other European countries had already established settlements in other areas and were set on becoming the **dominant** power in North America. France had a strong foothold in Canada, Louisiana, and the Mississippi River Valley. Spain's empire in North America included a huge portion of the western lands, and parts of Louisiana and Mississippi. Spain also controlled part of what would become the state of Florida. Competition for control of North America was one of the events that led to wars in Europe, four of which spilled over into Colonial America.

King William's War (1689–1697)

In Europe, it was called the "War of the League of Augsburg." In the colonies, it was known as "King William's War," named for King William III of England. It was a war between Britain and France for world power, control of North America, and **monopoly** of the fur trade.

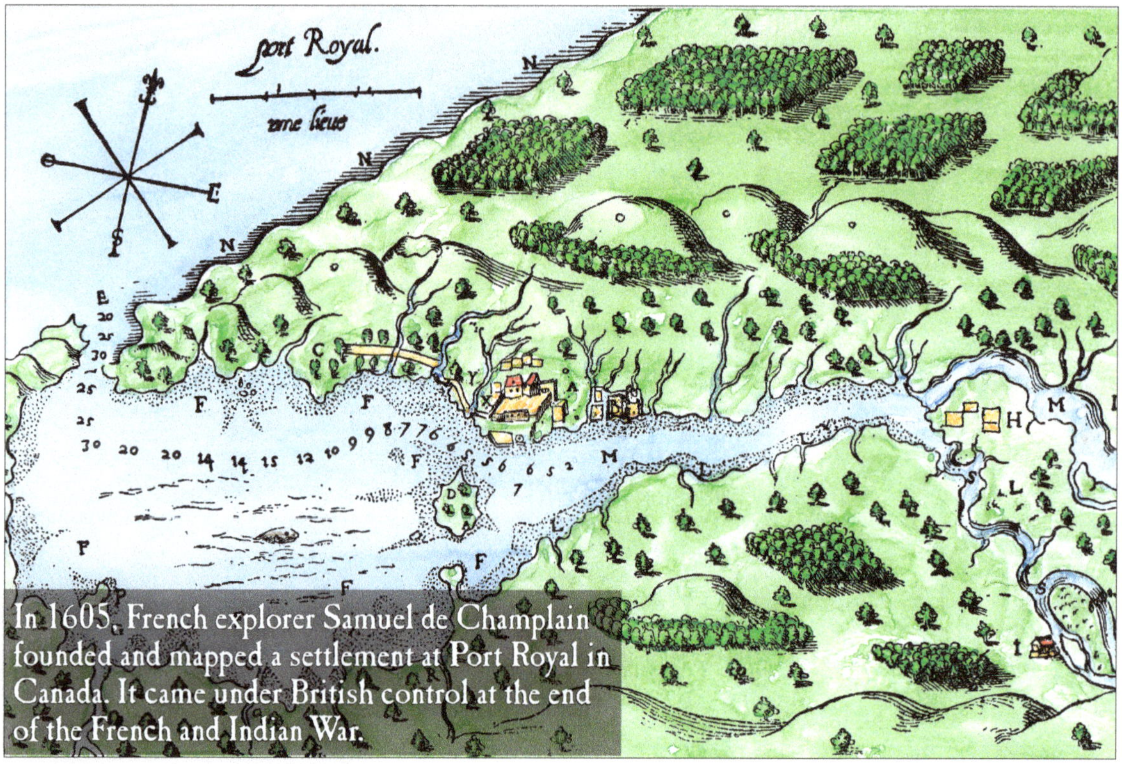

In 1605, French explorer Samuel de Champlain founded and mapped a settlement at Port Royal in Canada. It came under British control at the end of the French and Indian War.

Competition over control of North America was already causing tension between British and French colonists when Britain declared war on France in 1689. In the colonies, King William's War started with a series of attacks on British colonial settlements in New Hampshire that were led by the French and their Native American allies. More attacks on settlements in New York and Maine followed. British colonists and their Native American allies struck back by attacking the French settlement of Port-Royal, in French Acadia (present-day Annapolis Royal, Nova Scotia). They then sent a fleet of ships and soldiers to bombard and attack Quebec, hoping to overtake the French stronghold. They failed. Quebec remained under French control.

King William's War ended with the Treaty of Ryswick in 1697. For the colonies, nothing had officially changed. The British and the French maintained control of the areas of North America that they'd previously claimed. But the battle for power would soon resume, and it would once again involve the colonies.

Queen Anne's War (1702–1713)

Queen Anne's War, known in Europe as the War of Spanish Succession, broke out in 1702. As was King William's War, it was a battle for power. And in it, Britain, the Netherlands, and several German states were allies against France and Spain.

In North America, Queen Anne's War was fought as far south as Florida and north into Canada. One of the earliest conflicts took place in Florida, when South Carolina's British forces attacked the Spanish stronghold of St. Augustine. The Spanish held on, and the British finally retreated—but they burned St. Augustine to the ground as they left.

Farther north, border raids between the French, along with their Native American allies, and the British and their Native American allies, maintained a steady pace. Troops from New England and a fleet of British ships attacked and conquered the French Acadian city of Port-Royal.

Queen Anne's War ended in 1713. Under the Treaty of Utrecht, the French lands called Acadia became the British province of Nova Scotia. Britain also won Newfoundland and the Hudson Bay region from France and shipping rights in the Caribbean Sea.

King George's War (1744–1748)

The prelude to King George's War (in Europe, the War of Austrian Succession) began in the Caribbean in 1739, when Spanish **privateers** boarded a British ship and reportedly cut off Captain Robert Jenkins's ear. When called to testify about the incident before a committee of the House of Commons, Jenkins displayed the severed ear.

The 1758 French surrender of Fort Louisbourg to the British gave the British access to the St. Lawrence River and to Quebec, a French stronghold.

With its control of Florida and much of the Caribbean, Spain was a threat to many of the Southern Colonies. James Oglethorpe, governor of the Georgia colony, employed a combination of troops in an attempt to take St. Augustine. His attempt—just as South Carolina's had years before—failed.

The War of Jenkins' Ear (1739) eventually merged into the larger King George's War, which erupted in 1744. This time France and Spain were allies against Britain. France kicked off the war in North America with a failed attack on Nova Scotia. In **retaliation**, the British and the colonies attacked Louisbourg, a French fort on Cape Breton Island. Louisbourg was heavily armed because it guarded the entrance to the St. Lawrence River. The river was an important water route for transporting both goods and people. A British fleet set up a **blockade** of the river while a 4,000-citizen militia from New England besieged it. After two months, the fort surrendered. It was the greatest victory colonial forces had ever won.

But in the Treaty of Aix-la-Chapelle (Treaty of Aachen), which ended King George's War in 1748, the British returned Louisbourg to the French in exchange for the Indian city of Madras, which the French had captured. The colonies were so furious that Britain agreed to **reimburse** them for the money they'd spent.

French And Indian War (1754–1763)

In 1753, Britain was in control of the thirteen colonies. But beyond the Appalachian Mountains was a large area of land that stretched from Louisiana through the Mississippi Valley and up to the Great Lakes and into Canada—and both Britain and France wanted to settle it. The area was called "New France," but no one agreed on what part belonged to which country.

The French had built a string of forts in the upper Ohio River Valley—territory that the Virginia colony claimed belonged to it. Virginia's governor ordered George Washington, a young lieutenant colonel, and a troop of

In 1754, George Washington's soldiers, along with Native American allies, attacked a French encampment in Pennsylvania. The attack sparked the French and Indian War.

Virginia militia on an expedition. Their job was to force the French to give up Fort Duquesne, in what is now Pittsburgh. It didn't work. After a skirmish with a small French patrol, Washington and his troops had to quickly build a stockade for protection: Fort Necessity. Eventually, a larger French force arrived and attacked the fort. Washington and his men ran out of ammunition, and at the end of a day's fighting, Washington surrendered the fort.

When Britain's prime minister learned of the defeat at Fort Necessity, he ordered "secret" strikes in retaliation. But the plan didn't remain secret. France got wind of it, and Britain and France officially declared war on each other.

The Seven Years War, a global conflict known in America as the French and Indian War, officially began in 1756, with France, Austria, and Russia, among others, squaring off against Britain and Prussia. But in the colonies, it had started two years earlier (1754). Once again, Britain and France were fighting for control of North American territories.

The war didn't start well for Britain. In 1755, a force of about 2,200, including two regiments sent from Britain and militiamen from Virginia and North Carolina, set out to take Fort Duquesne. British commander Major General Edward Braddock had years of experience. Yet his battles took place on the open terrain of European battlefields and employed European-style fighting with troops in close formation—not the type of fighting he would encounter in North America. French soldiers, along with their Native American allies, used the forests and rough terrain as cover and ambushed Braddock and his troops. "Scarce an officer or soldier," wrote one of the participants, "can say they ever saw at one time six of the Enemy and the greatest part never saw a single man."

The war had become a disaster for the British. Braddock was killed, the troops scattered, and more defeats followed. British troops had learned some "frontier" tactics, but they didn't use them as often or as well as the French did. After Braddock's defeat, the British did not abandon their old way of fighting, but they realized that they had to work harder at adapting to the forested, rocky terrain of North America. They began to use some of their troops as scouts and skirmishers. Instead of the British red coats, these troops dressed

The French thought they were secure atop the cliffs of Quebec, but British troops scaled the cliffs in the dead of night and took Quebec in 1759.

in brown and green to camouflage themselves in the forests. They recruited more colonial forces and Native American allies who not only knew their way around the territory, but also knew how to fight in it.

Soon a new British prime minister, William Pitt, began pouring money and troops into the war effort. Canada became the main battleground. Together with militia forces from different colonies, the British began to turn things around. They recaptured Louisbourg, which had been taken from them

Battle of Quebec (1759)

In his account of the Battle of Quebec, a British solder wrote:

"On the 14th we landed, at break of Day, and immediately attacked and routed the Enemy...We then took Post on the Plains of Abraham, whither M. Montcalm (on hearing that we had landed, for he did not expect us) hasted with his whole Army... to give us Battle."

The Plains of Abraham—named for Abraham Martin, a fisherman—was a plateau atop the cliff overlooking Quebec. A force of infantrymen led by Colonel William Howe, who would later command British forces during the American Revolution, scaled the cliff to the plains at night. At dawn, forces led by General James Wolfe had "taken post" on the plains, ready to face off with the French forces commanded by General Louis-Joseph de Montcalm-Gozon, marquis de Montcalm.

The forces were matched in manpower with approximately 4,500 soldiers each. According to the soldier's account, the French began firing when they were fifty yards away. The British waited "as it was General Wolfe's express Orders not to fire till they came within twenty Yards of us ..." then unleashed a **volley** that broke the French line. More volleys followed, the French retreated, and "The Enemy lost in the Engagement ..."

General Wolfe died on the battlefield. General Montcalm died of his wounds the next day. The British lay siege to Quebec and the French surrendered the territory in the Treaty of Paris (1763), which ended the French and Indian War in North America. Colonial forces in the Revolutionary War would unsuccessfully try to take Quebec from the British.

in the Treaty of Utrecht, which ended Queen Anne's War. They captured forts in Ontario and northern New York and cut off the French from some of their main supply centers on the Great Lakes.

One of the captured forts was Fort Niagara, located at the mouth of western New York's Niagara River. It was an important gateway to both the Great Lakes and the western part of North America. During the first few years of the French and Indian War, the French and their Native American allies used the fort as a base to conduct raids on the British, especially in Pennsylvania.

In May 1759, British forces set out to capture Fort Niagara, and in June, during the battle of La Belle Famille, they succeeded. The French surrendered the fort and Britain then used it as a storehouse for supplies. Expeditions left from Fort Niagara to establish military outposts farther west. The fort would remain under British control throughout the Revolutionary War.

By 1760, Britain had taken control of the entire North American frontier. The French and Indian War ended with the Treaty of Paris on February 10, 1763. Spain surrendered its control of Florida, and France surrendered all of its North American territory to Britain.

Chapter Five

Celebration and Rebellion

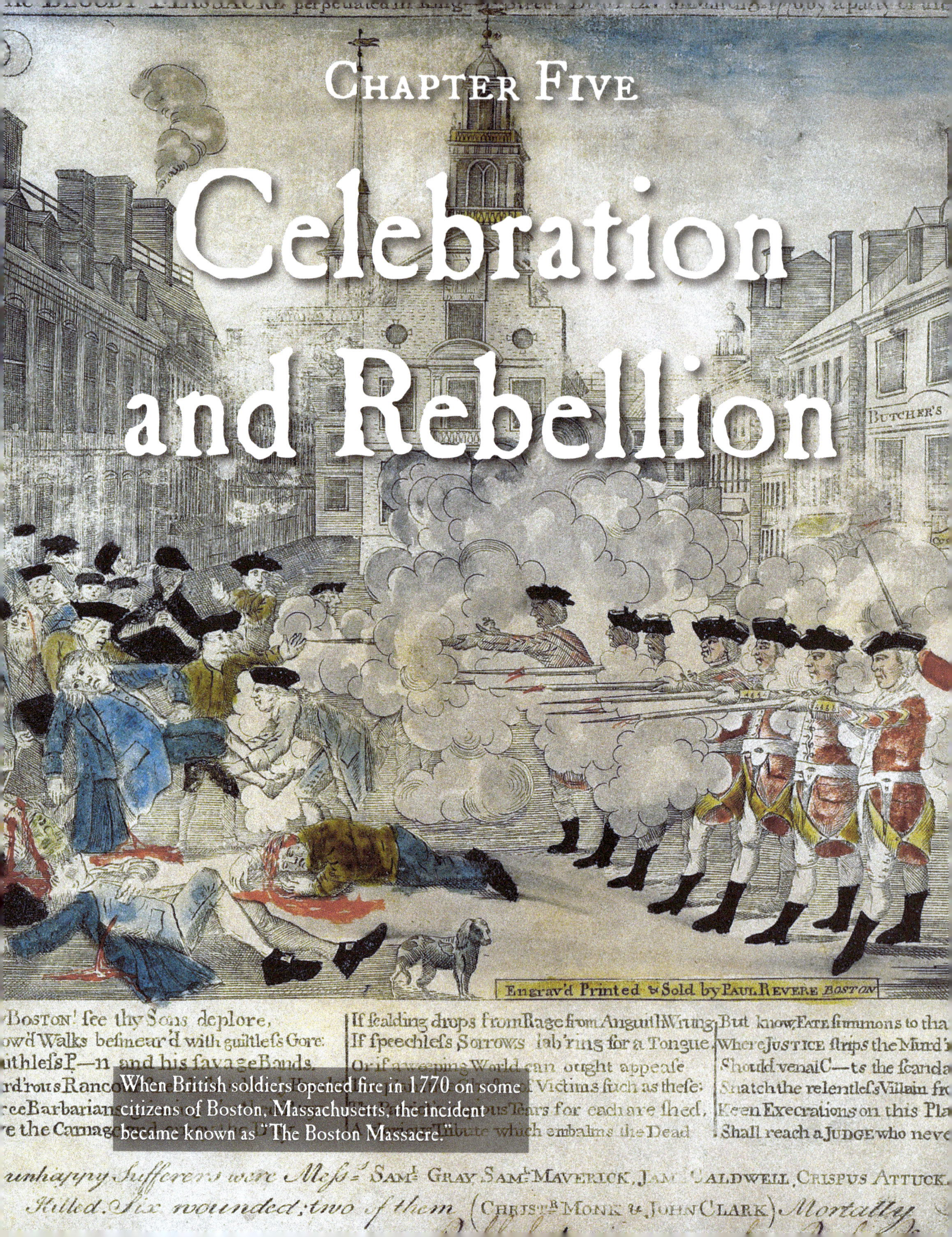

When British soldiers opened fire in 1770 on some citizens of Boston, Massachusetts, the incident became known as "The Boston Massacre."

"I can see no reason to doubt but that the imposition of taxes, whether on trade, or on houses, on ships, on real or personal, fixed or floating property, in the colonies is absolutely irreconcilable with the rights of the colonists as British subjects."
—James Otis in The Rights of the British Colonies Asserted and Proved, 1764

Bells rang on both sides of the Atlantic. Fireworks lit the skies and cannons boomed in celebration of Britain's victory in the French and Indian War. Benjamin Franklin wrote letters of congratulation to British leaders. In churches throughout the colonies, ministers gave joyful thanks that life would now be peaceful. "Now commences the Era of our Quiet Enjoyment of those Liberties which our Fathers purchased with the Toil of their whole Lives, their Treasure, their Blood."

One group that did not celebrate was the Native Americans, especially the tribes living in the Great Lakes region. That land was no longer French territory. According to the Treaty of Paris, it had become part of the British Empire. The tribes in that area had established a decent relationship with the French, who were there mostly to hunt and trade fur. Although many Native Americans had been allies of the British, they were cautious about what would happen next.

The relationship between Native Americans and the British got off to a poor start. Major General Jeffrey Amherst, the commander of British forces in

Fed up with colonists taking over their land, often by force, many Native Americans believed they had to fight back or lose their way of life.

North America, was in charge of organizing Britain's vast North American empire. Even before the French and Indian War had ended, Amherst ordered an end to giving gifts to the chiefs of Native American allies. This practice—part of the Native American culture—had been followed throughout the colonies for more than a hundred years. It was a gesture of respect that helped maintain peaceful relations. Amherst, who felt that he no longer needed Native American support, viewed the gifts as bribes. He also decided to limit the amount of gunpowder Native Americans could receive in trade, "since nothing can be so **impolitick** as to furnish them with the means of accomplishing the Evil which is so much Dreaded."

Despite their promise to withdraw troops from the region, the British maintained a presence in strongholds such as Fort Pitt, which was large enough to hold a thousand men. Finally, the British urged already land-hungry colonists from east of the Appalachian Mountains to move into the tribal lands to tend trading posts, and build settlements and farms. Native Americans believed they were being treated as conquered people, not as partners, allies, or neighbors—they had been betrayed. For the Native Americans, the British troops, and the colonists, there would be no "Era of Quiet Enjoyment."

Pontiac's Rebellion 1763–1766

In May 1763, Pontiac, an Ottawa leader, led a coalition of Native Americans toward Fort Detroit. Armed with concealed weapons, their goal was to attack and capture the fort from the British. They had an even bigger goal than taking the fort: to completely expel British troops from Native American territory. And war, they believed, was the only way to do it.

Word of the surprise attack got out, so Pontiac did not attack. But he and his men lay siege to the fort, killing soldiers and settlers in the area. It was just the beginning. In less than two months, the alliance of Native Americans had taken eight British forts. They also began a series of raids on settlements. Panicked and outnumbered, settlers fled or were killed.

In April, 1763, the Ottawa leader Pontiac persuaded members of several Native American tribes to join in a rebellion against the British.

Ruthless Warfare

Native American attacks on settlers seemed **ruthless** to the British. A British general who fought in Pontiac's Rebellion wrote, "The frontiers of Pennsylvania, Maryland, and Virginia, were immediately overrun with scalping parties, marking their way with blood and devastation wherever they came."

Meanwhile, what British General Jeffrey Amherst had suggested could be defined as an early form of biological warfare: the intentional spread of smallpox. The deadly disease had sickened and killed many Native Americans before. But after hearing about smallpox-infected blankets being given to Native Americans, he wrote to one of his officers: "You will do well to try to inoculate the Indians by means of blankets, as well as to try every other method that can serve to **extirpate** this **execrable** race." Whether Amherst's thought was carried out remains uncertain.

Pontiac's Rebellion lasted for months and was finally settled with negotiations. Among other things, Native Americans agreed to return captives they had taken, and the British agreed to respect the tradition of giving gifts and resume trading gunpowder. And through the Royal Proclamation of 1763 (issued on October 7), Britain's King George III made it clear to the colonists that they had "**forthwith** to remove themselves" from west of the Appalachians.

The proclamation created a huge Native American reserve of land—land the colonists wanted. Many of the colonists had fought for, and with, the British during the French and Indian War. They'd established **homesteads** and started farms, and then were forced to flee during Pontiac's Rebellion. Now, according to the proclamation, they could not to return.

The proclamation also created resentment among wealthy colonists. Men such as George Washington, Thomas Jefferson, and Patrick Henry had made investments in companies that sold large tracts of land west of the Appalachians. Because of the proclamation, the companies, and the men, suffered financial losses.

In spite of the proclamation, the British troops did not stop many settlers from moving west—and these colonists took their resentment with them.

Troops And Taxes

Britain was deeply in debt. Winning the French and Indian War had cost an enormous amount of money. Its debt stood at over 150 million pounds and the yearly interest on it was more than four million pounds. To oversee and protect its vast new territory in North America was going to cost even more. Where would the money come from?

The answer to this question was obvious to Britain: the money should come from the colonies. Colonists needed to start paying their fair share. After all, Britain had essentially bankrolled the war, kept the colonies safely under British rule, and protected them from Native American uprisings. Britain even allowed 10,000 of its troops to remain stationed in North America, in case they were needed. And those troops had to be housed and fed. So on March 24, 1765, the British Parliament passed the Quartering Act, which outlined the locations and conditions in which British soldiers were to find room and board in the American colonies.

The Quartering Act of 1765 stated that colonies must house British soldiers in barracks and **public houses**. If there weren't enough of those accommodations, the troops had to be quartered in inns, alehouses, barns, unoccupied houses, and other buildings. The Act also listed **provisions** the

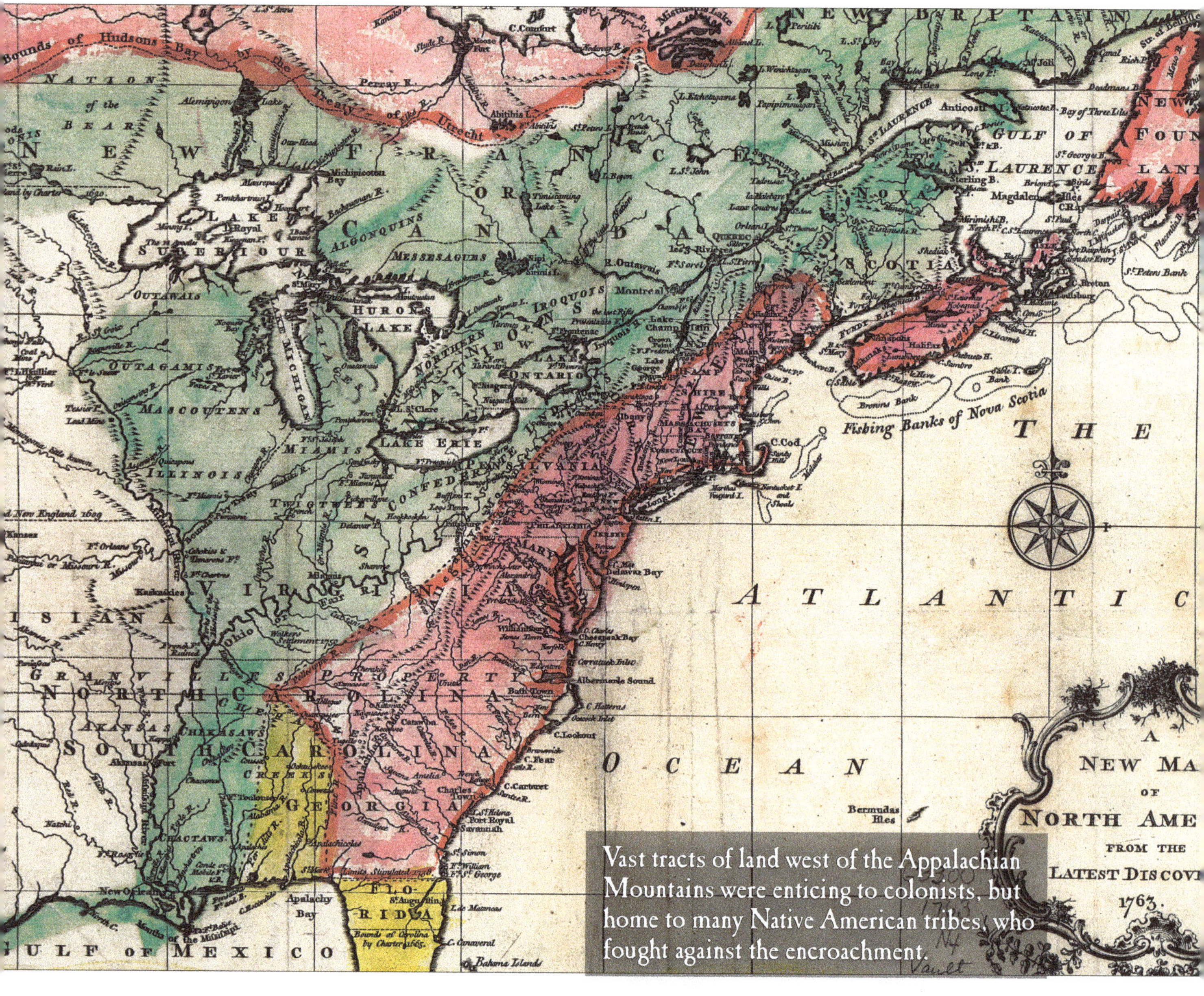

Vast tracts of land west of the Appalachian Mountains were enticing to colonists, but home to many Native American tribes, who fought against the encroachment.

Acts of Parliament

The British Parliament passed several Acts starting in the 1760s. Among them were the Sugar Act, the Stamp Act, the Tea Act, and the Townshend Act. Each served as a way to raise money for the British treasury and to help pay for British troops stationed in the colonies. Colonists grumbled from the beginning, especially about the Stamp Act of 1765.

Earlier levies imposed by the Parliament taxed imported goods. The Stamp Act, however, was a direct tax on the property and goods owned by the colonists. Newspapers, diplomas, almanacs, pamphlets, wills, dice, playing cards—all had to bear a stamp to prove that the tax had been paid.

British manufacturers generated sales by appealing to American consumers, despite political differences. This teapot and others like it sold well in the colonies.

The grumbling in the colonies turned to shouts. The shouts turned to protests, some of which were violent. The Sons of Liberty, an organization of shopkeepers, printers, and businessmen, formed to protest the Act. Even though neither the colonial militia nor the British troops became involved, Britain sat up and took notice. Although Britain repealed the Stamp Act in 1766, it still claimed power over the colonies.

colonists should supply, such as cooking utensils, firewood, bedding, candles, cider, and beer. The colonies, however, held a different opinion.

Colonists supplied provisions to British troops during the French and Indian War, but the war was over. There was no need for such a large number of troops to remain in the colonies. The militia and the provincial troops could handle safety issues and emergencies. In the past, militiamen could quickly be called for action if there was a crisis. When the fighting was over, the militia disbanded until the next crisis came along. In fact, many colonists thought their own militia could do a much better job than the British troops—and 10,000 British troops represented a standing army.

Prior to the French and Indian War, there had been no formal standing army in the colonies—and the colonists didn't want one now.

A second Quartering Act in 1774 expanded on the first of 1765: British troops could now be quartered in any occupied home.

Chapter Six

A New Battle, A New Army

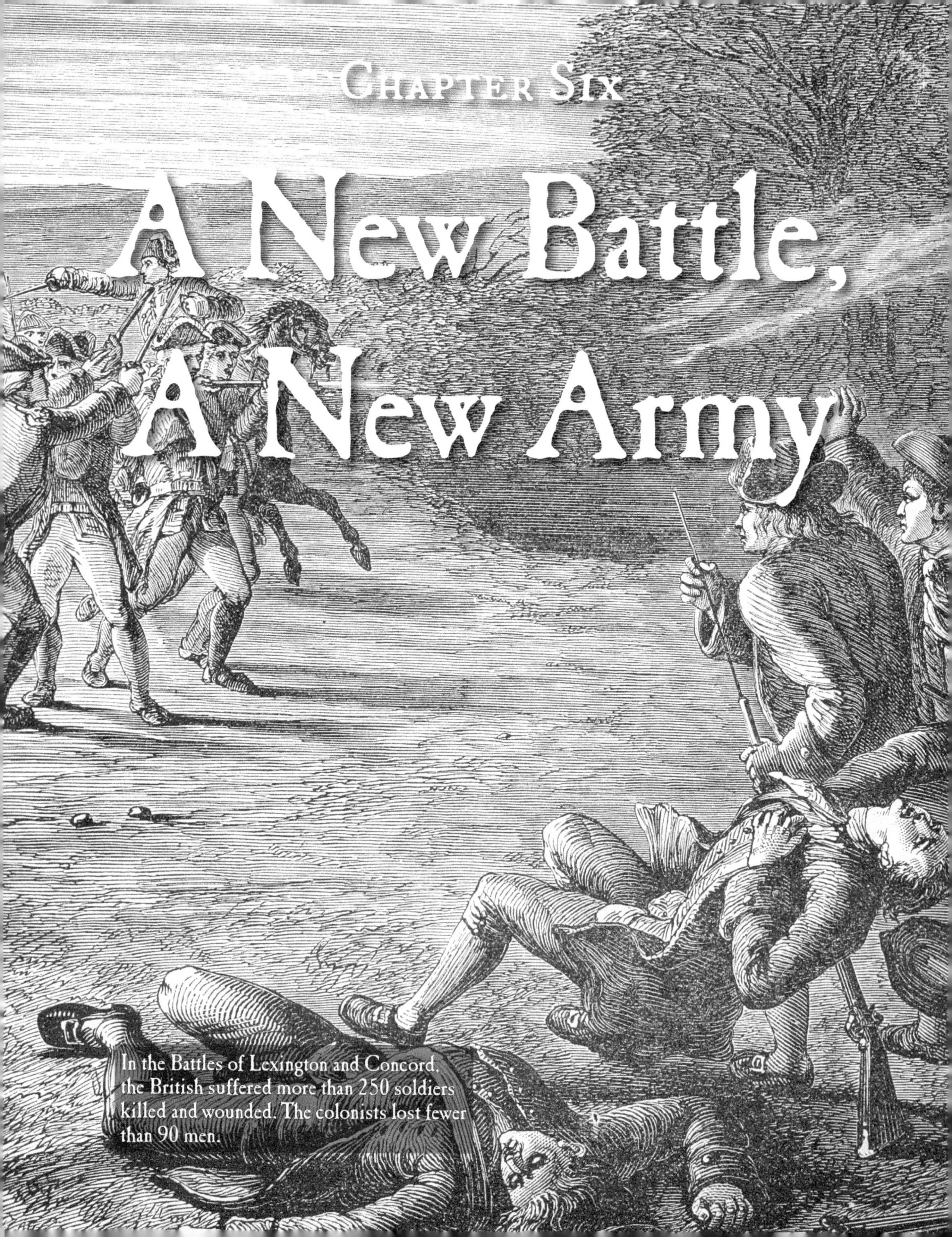

In the Battles of Lexington and Concord, the British suffered more than 250 soldiers killed and wounded. The colonists lost fewer than 90 men.

"Without a respectable navy—alas America."

—John Paul Jones in a letter to Robert Morris, October 17, 1776

Colonists were fed up with Britain's unfair taxes. They had no representation or vote in the British Parliament and argued that they couldn't be taxed without their consent—which they hadn't given. Britain strongly disagreed.

Lexington And Concord

Colonial militia had hidden a large stash of weapons in Concord, Massachusetts. British general Thomas Gage was ordered by the British government to seize the arsenal, disarm the militia, and to capture Patriot leaders Samuel Adams and John Hancock, who were hiding in the nearby town of Lexington. Around 5 a.m. on April 19, 1775, seven hundred British soldiers marched into Lexington. They met seventy-seven minutemen, who had been alerted to the invasion by riders Paul Revere and William Dawes, on the town's **common green**. Shots were fired. Although the minutemen had slowed them down, the British took Lexington. By the time the British reached Concord, an overwhelming force of 2,000 minutemen had gathered in waiting. The minutemen held back at

Disguised as Native Americans, merchants protested the Tea Act by dumping 342 chests of tea into the sea.

The Tea Act 1773

In 1773, the British Parliament passed the Tea Act, a bill designed to rescue British-owned East India Company from bankruptcy by greatly lowering the tea tax it paid to the British government. This resulted in the company's **de facto** monopoly on the American tea trade. The price of tea was lowered so much that colonists couldn't afford to buy it from any other source, including other colonial merchants. The response of some of the colonists was to dump the tea into Boston Harbor.

The British reacted to the "Tea Party" by closing the port of Boston, placing the city under military control, and appointing a British general as the military governor of Massachusetts.

Representatives from the colonies met in the First Continental Congress in Philadelphia and agreed to send a letter to the British government, stating the colonies' grievances. Britain responded by declaring that the colonies were in rebellion. The colonies agreed. They had not yet declared independence, but they were heading in that direction.

first, and the British destroyed what stores of weapons were left. As the British marched out of Concord, the minutemen attacked and forced the British to retreat. When the smoke cleared, the British had lost more than 200 men. The minutemen had lost about ninety.

The Continental Army

When George Washington arrived in Boston in July 1775, the colonial forces had just fought their first major Revolutionary War battle at nearby Bunker Hill. Although they surprised the British with their fighting tactics, they lost the battle.

The Battle of Bunker Hill, 1775, actually took place on Breed's Hill in Boston. Although British troops were the ultimate victors, colonial troops trapped the British and lay siege to the city.

Earlier, the colonial troops had won a small victory at Fort Ticonderoga. Located on the edge of Lake Champlain in the north of New York, it guarded an important route between the colonies and Britain's northern provinces in Canada. The British had captured the fort from the French during the French and Indian War, and the colonies knew it could be used as a way for British forces to invade from the north. To block such a takeover, and to use the route to invade Canada themselves, colonists decided to seize the fort.

In May 1775, Ethan Allen and the Green Mountain Boys, a militia group from Vermont, attacked Fort Ticonderoga. With only forty-eight British soldiers stationed there, it was a bloodless win—the first official American victory of the Revolutionary War. But the fort's capture gave the colonies more than their first victory—inside it were cannons, guns, and ammunition desperately needed by the Continental Army in Boston.

Boston was under siege in the fall of 1775. The Continental Army had very little artillery except a few pieces left behind by the British after the Battle of Bunker Hill. And George Washington knew that he needed cannons if he was going to free the city.

Henry Knox, a major general in the army, had an idea: Take troops to Fort Ticonderoga and return to Boston with the artillery that Ethan Allen and the Green Mountain Boys had captured. Washington quickly agreed and sent Knox to New York, saying that, "The want of them [cannons] is so great that no trouble or expense must be spared to obtain them."

Trouble was definitely not spared. First the heavy cannons had to be disassembled, then more than a thousand pounds of artillery had to be hauled the 300 miles to Boston in the freezing cold of winter. With boats, rafts, horses, "forty-two exceeding strong sleds" and "eighty yoke of oxen," Knox's troops forged icy rivers and crossed snowy forests. His "noble train of artillery" reached Boston in January 1776. The guns were set up so they could strike British troops and ships. Rather than attack, the British withdrew, and Boston returned to American forces.

But the British were far from defeated, and the second Continental Congress met in Philadelphia and authorized the creation of the Continental Army, with George Washington as its commander. Washington believed that only a strong, organized army could stand up to the British, who had more soldiers, more weapons, more money, and superior organization. Militia members were trained, but not like regular soldiers. They served for short periods, and then returned to their homes. In fact, they insisted on doing so once a battle had ended. They had

Commissioned by George Washington to prey on British ships, the schooner *Hannah* was the first armed vessel to sail under the authority of the Continental Congress.

families to provide for, crops to tend, and shops to manage. But if the colonies were going to battle the British and win, Washington believed that they needed a force of disciplined, professional soldiers.

Washington organized the New England troops into three divisions, six brigades, thirty-eight regiments, and began to form the Continental Army. But creating that army meant more than appointing brigades and regiments. An army needed money for weapons, food, clothing, and housing, but the Continental Congress couldn't levy taxes directly on the colonies, because there was no centralized federal government. The Continental Congress had to ask the colonies to contribute, which they were reluctant to do because they had their own militias to support. Maintaining a fighting force would prove a difficult task, one that never really ended.

Land forces weren't all that was needed. At the time, Britain had the most powerful navy in the world. British ships were prepared to attack colonial settlements, as well as deliver supplies and artillery to British troops stationed in the colonies.

The colonial forces, however, had no navy. Washington asked the Continental Congress to establish one, but many delegates to the Congress were reluctant to do so. A permanent American fleet would be costly, of little or no use to the colonies, and could not compete with Britain's superior naval force. One delegate commented that it was the "maddest idea in the world." Meanwhile, Washington took matters into his own hands and hired privately owned **schooners** to sail off the Massachusetts coast and intercept British ships laden with munitions and supplies. These schooners became known as "George Washington's Navy."

In early October 1775, word reached Congress that two British ships were en route to Quebec to supply the British forces. Congress approved a plan to outfit two armed vessels to cruise along the east coast and intercept any ships bringing supplies to the British army. Shortly after, the delegates received a letter from Washington, telling them that he'd hired several schooners for the same reason. With that, Congress voted to establish a Continental Navy, and appointed a committee to oversee the purchase of the new navy's first ships.

The navy started out with seven ships. But throughout the war, more than fifty fleets were tasked to disrupt British trade routes in the Caribbean and shipments of supplies in the North Atlantic. The Continental Navy never came close to matching the British fleet in numbers. It did, however, capture or destroy many of Britain's ships, a move that forced the British to use their warships to protect their trade routes. Just as important, the navy seized British supplies that were desperately needed by the Continental Army.

Uniforms and Cockades

When first organized, the new army had no uniforms. Because funding to support the troops was minimal, many of the regular enlisted soldiers were often lucky to have warm coats and shoes without holes. Still, Washington believed that uniforms were an important part of a professional army: they gave a sense of order and pride.

In 1775, the Continental Congress chose brown as the uniform's official color. But not all troops wore brown. Many local companies had already chosen different colors. Blue was popular, especially with officers. Eventually, blue became the official color of the uniform coat. The color of the coats' linings and **facings** varied as a way to identify the rank of the person wearing it.

The hunting shirt worn by expert marksmen from some of the colonies became the field dress of most of the army. According to Washington, "No dress can be cheaper, nor more convenient, as the wearer may be cool in warm weather and warm in cool weather ... Besides which it is a dress justly supposed to carry no small terror to the enemy, who think every such person a complete marksman."

Even with uniforms, it was often difficult for soldiers to tell who was in charge on the battlefield. A cockade—a wide knot or rosette of ribbon worn on the hat—helped solve the problem. The color of a cockade helped soldiers identify their commanders by rank. In the early years, field officers wore red or pink, captains wore buff or yellow, and junior officers wore green. Commanders eventually adopted the black cockade, and later, when France entered the war on the side of the colonies, black-and-white.

An officer of the Continental Navy, John Paul Jones took the fight to the enemy during the Revolutionary War with daring raids along the British coast.

Chapter Seven

A Continental Army at War

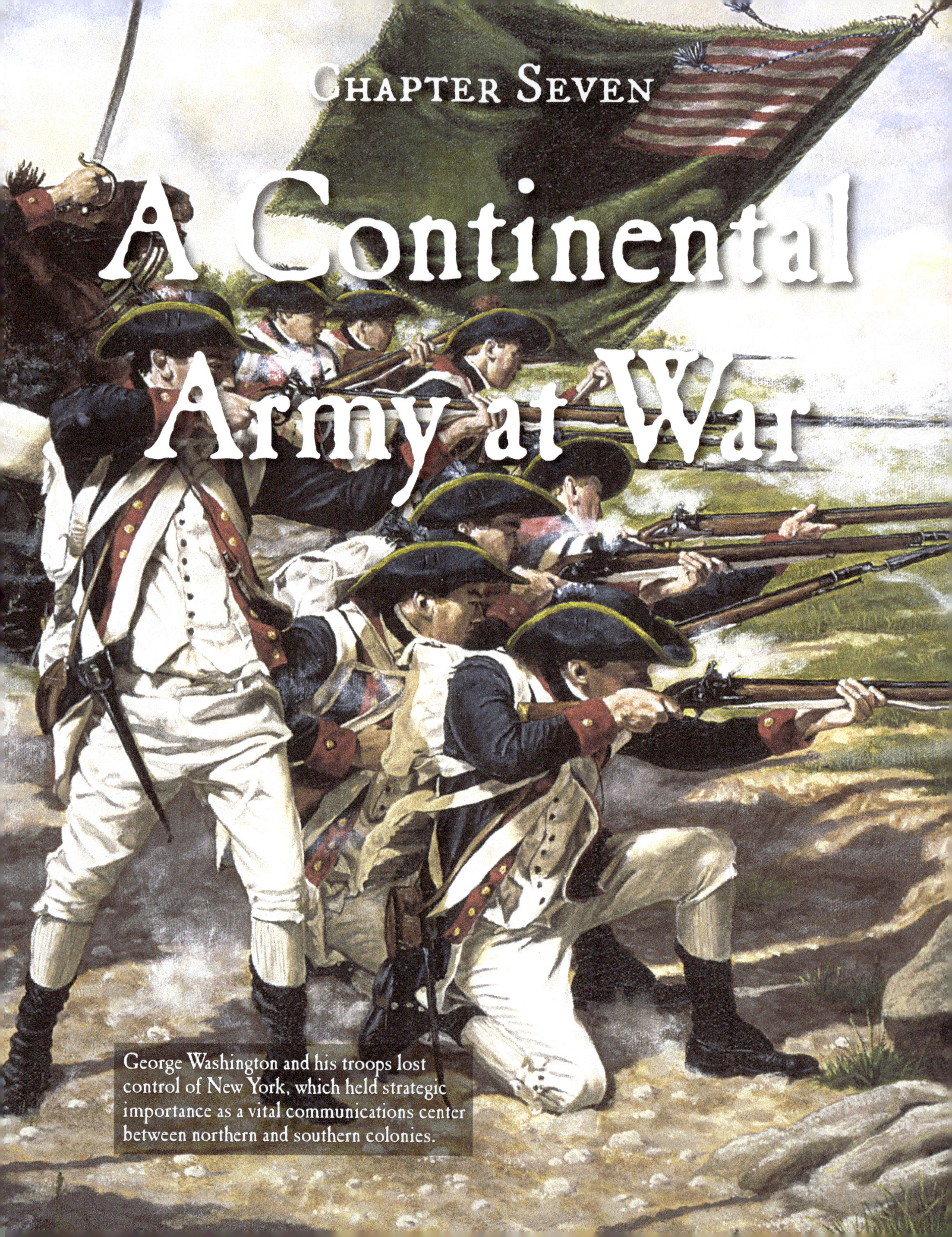

George Washington and his troops lost control of New York, which held strategic importance as a vital communications center between northern and southern colonies.

"It is not a field of a few acres of ground, but a cause, we are defending, and whether we defeat the enemy in one battle, or by degrees, the consequences will be the same."
—Thomas Paine in *The Crisis*, 1777

The first major battle of the Revolutionary War took place in 1776. Thousands of British troops advanced into New York and attempted to trap the Americans in Brooklyn. American troops held off as long as they could, but were finally forced to retreat. The British had taken New York. It was not a good start for Washington and the Continental Army. But even though the battle had been lost, the Continental Army proved that it was willing to fight and could fight well. But the soldiers still required more training.

Most of the regular soldiers who served in the Continental Army were young and inexperienced. Thousands were under the age of twenty. Some were as young as thirteen when they joined. Sixteen was the minimum age, but fifteen-year-olds could join if their parents gave consent.

In the beginning, men and boys enlisted for one year. Soon it was changed to two. By 1776, soldiers in the regular force had to sign up for three years of service. In 1777, Washington persuaded Congress that enlistments should be for the duration of the war—in other words, for however long the war lasted.

Color Line

When Washington took command of the Continental Army, Congress put a stop to further recruitment of African American soldiers, despite the fact that they had fought at the battles of Lexington, Concord, and Bunker Hill. Yet the Royal Governor of Georgia promised freedom to all slaves who would join the British troops and fight against the colonies. At the chance for freedom, thousands of black men enlisted.

The Continental Congress then changed its mind and again allowed free blacks to enlist. By 1778, a few Southern slave-holding states granted freedom to slaves who served in the Revolutionary War. Five thousand black men served in the Continental Army, and hundreds more served on the sea.

African Americans served in almost every Revolutionary War battle. The man on the left is from the 1st Rhode Island Regiment, and was said to have served at Yorktown in Virginia.

Recruits received a bounty, or bonus, for enlisting. Service was voluntary at first, but as the war continued, Congress told the states that they had to fill quotas. Drafted men with money could pay a substitute to take their places. Many servants and apprentices became soldiers this way.

The Continental Army not only lacked experience, its soldiers were outnumbered. Washington knew this and had no visions of winning the war in one knockout battle. According to his aide Alexander Hamilton, the plan was "to take advantage of favorable opportunities, and waste and defeat the enemy by **piecemeal**."

Washington created a "favorable opportunity" when he and his army, including horses and wagons, crossed the icy Delaware River during a snowstorm on Christmas night in 1776. Armies usually made camp during the winter months, but Washington was determined to gain ground after losing the battle in New York. Riding along the lines of the troops, encouraging them to continue on, he led his army from Pennsylvania into Trenton, a small town in New Jersey. There, they surprised and overpowered a Hessian force of about 1,400 men. The Hessians, from the German area of Hesse-Cassel, were being paid to fight for the British. The battle was short-lived, and the victorious Americans moved on to take Princeton, New Jersey. After the humiliating defeat in New York, the New Jersey victories gave a huge boost to the Continental Army's morale.

But over the summer of 1777, the British won battles in Pennsylvania, and then occupied the city of Philadelphia, where the Continental Congress met. The Congress had to flee the city and relocate to York, Pennsylvania. By the winter, when the American troops made their camp at Valley Forge, Pennsylvania, morale was low. Supplies of meat and bread were short, leaving

Small but successful battles in New Jersey in 1776 led to increased confidence in George Washington's leadership and a decrease in desertions.

Conditions were so bad at Valley Forge that George Washington feared that the army would either starve or disband in order to survive.

Short Rations

What have you for your dinner boys?
"Nothing but Fire Cake and Water, Sir."
At night, "Gentlemen the Supper is ready."
What is your Supper Lads? "Fire Cake and Water, Sir."

Soldiers had to eat in spite of regularly unavailable rations. Fire cakes were globs of flour mixed with water and salt, if there was any. The mixture was flattened into cakes, and baked on a rock warmed by the ashes from a fire. A fire cake was hard, dry, and tasteless, and required plenty of water to wash it down.

soldiers to forage for food in the forests. Long marches had destroyed almost all of the soldiers' shoes. Supplies of blankets were scarce, and there were rarely any replacements for tattered clothing. Officers and regular soldiers had not been paid.

Pennsylvania was freezing cold. The soldiers built log huts for protection from the harsh weather. This meant hauling logs, which were also in short supply, without the aid of farm animals. There was a lack of proper tools and warm clothing to wear while working. Eventually the soldiers completed about 2,000 huts, each housing about twelve men. The huts provided shelter for the soldiers, but did little to fill their stomachs or mend their tattered shoes.

As if all this weren't enough, Washington knew that his army still needed to improve greatly if they were to win the war. Enter Baron von Steuben.

A Stronger Army

Baron Friedrich Wilhelm Augustus von Steuben was an out-of-work military professional from Prussia. He offered his services to the American army and eventually became its Inspector General. He arrived at Valley Forge in February 1778. His job was to drill the soldiers and turn them into a better-trained army.

Baron von Steuben trained the Continental Army and commanded a division in the Battle of Yorktown. His men were in the trenches when the British offered to surrender.

It has been said that because von Steuben didn't speak English, he tried to give his instructions in sign language. When that didn't work, he would lose his temper and begin to curse. Whether he swore or not, von Steuben taught the troops new and better ways to maneuver on the battlefield and to handle their firearms.

Ezra Selden, adjutant and captain in the First Connecticut Regiment, described the training sessions with von Steuben in a letter to Doctor Samuel Mather of Lyme, Connecticut:

"Valley Forge, May 15, 1778. Our Army is at present very busy and intent upon a new mode of exercise pointed by Major General Baron Stuben from Poland. His knowledge in discipline is very great, his method of maneuvering is very difficult; but mostly satisfactory, he never informs what is to be done in future; but gives lessons and we practice untill he gives new directions."

Baron von Steuben also insisted on better sanitation in the camp. To prevent contamination of food supplies, he instructed, kitchens should be on the opposite side of the camp from latrines. Latrines should always be located on the downhill side of the camp so any run-off from the slop jars would flow away from the camp and be less likely to cause illness. The carcasses of animals should be tossed into the forest, instead of being allowed to decompose in the camp.

All of these instructions were to help prevent sickness and disease, which were rampant not only at Valley Forge, but everywhere throughout the war. More soldiers died from pneumonia, dysentery, typhus, and typhoid than in battles.

Battles of Saratoga (1777)

Baron von Steuben wasn't the only outside help the Continental Army received. Hoping that a colonial victory over Britain would give them a chance to recapture Canada, the French had been providing the colonies financial support almost since the beginning of the Revolutionary War. When the Americans defeated the British in the Battles of Saratoga (1777), France openly entered the war as an American ally, and sent close to 12,000 soldiers and 32,000 sailors to assist. Spain, a couple of years later, joined as an ally to the Americans and helped secure southern ports and supply lines.

The Battles of Saratoga were a turning point for the Continental Army. The British plan was to march south from northeastern New York and isolate all of New England from the Southern Colonies. There were two 1777 battles fought (September 19 and October 7), and the British lost both. Part of the reason was the local militia. When Washington realized that a major battle was shaping up, he sent troops north. He also said that any militia who could join the battle should do so. At the beginning of the war, Washington and most of his generals had a very low opinion of the colonial militia. They weren't well trained and they hurried home as soon as a fight was over. "To place any dependence upon militia is assuredly resting upon a broken staff," Washington wrote.

But the militia turned out to be stronger and more useful than anyone expected. They guarded camps, roads, and waterways. They were especially good at using their "guerilla" tactics of firing from behind boulders, buildings, fences, or trees, then quickly disappearing. Militia units kept smaller groups of British troops on the defensive by springing attacks almost daily. These skirmishes allowed divisions of the main army to move about the area without being attacked.

But the militia units were local groups who answered to local commanders, and there was very little coordination among them. In his farewell letter to the army, Washington urged that "the formation and discipline of the Militia of the Continent should be absolutely uniform, and that the same species of Arms, **Accoutrements** and Military Apparatus, should be introduced in every part of the United States."

Militia units were on hand when Britain decided to take the war to the Southern states late in 1778. The British thought there were many more loyalists—meaning colonists who did not want independence and would fight on Britain's side—in the South than in the North.

At first, it looked as if the Southern strategy might work when British forces conquered Savannah, Georgia. After bruising battles, they took

Charleston and then Camden, South Carolina. The Continental Army's regular troops couldn't seem to hold the British back, and the militia wasn't much help. But things began to look up for the Continental Army when Washington turned the Southern force over to a new commander, Nathaniel Greene. Greene used two generals to lead campaigns against the British forces. The generals knew how to command the troops, and how to use the militia. During the Battle of Cowpens, in South Carolina, British troops ran headlong into a barrage of musket fire from militia troops they thought had retreated. It was an overwhelming win for the Continental Army. And even though the British went on to victory at the Battle of Guilford Courthouse, in North Carolina, they were a much weaker force than when they'd started the Southern strategy.

Combined Forces

When King Louis XVI of France decided to send an expeditionary force to fight on the side of the colonies, he chose Count Rochambeau to lead it. Count Rochambeau, a French aristocrat, had earned an excellent reputation as a military strategist fighting in Europe during the War of Austrian Succession and the Seven Years' War. Rochambeau and approximately 5,000 troops landed in Newport, Rhode Island, on July 11, 1780.

Washington had hopes of taking New York. The British held it, but the Continental Army had it under siege. Then Rochambeau received word that a fleet of French ships and troops were headed for Chesapeake Bay, Virginia. Washington agreed with Rochambeau that a better plan was to take the war to the British in the South. The combined forces began their long march to Yorktown, Virginia, in August 1781.

Battle of Yorktown, 1781

British General Cornwallis left the Carolinas and took his troops to Yorktown, Virginia, to wait for reinforcements. Together, Washington and

Count Rochambeau marched their troops south from New York. A fleet of French ships with even more troops sailed in from the West Indies and surrounded the bay of Yorktown.

The British fought, but they lost the Battle of Yorktown, the final major engagement of the Revolutionary War. Even though the British still occupied several cities, they were worn down by the years of war. And British citizens were starting to object to paying taxes to support it.

After the British defeat at Yorktown, peace talks in Paris began in April 1782. In 1783, the Treaty of Paris put an official end to the war and recognized American independence. The preliminary articles of peace were signed on November 30, 1782. The treaty was not signed until September 3, 1783. The Continental Congress, which was temporarily situated in Annapolis, Maryland, ratified the treaty on January 14, 1784. After the treaty, the Continental Army was disbanded. On September 29, 1789, the last day of its first session, Congress passed an act to establish a permanent United States military force.

Announcing the British surrender, George Washington wrote: "I have the Honor to inform Congress, that a Reduction of the British Army under the Command of Lord Cornwallis, is most happily effected."

Glossary

accoutrements

An outfit or equipment, especially that of a soldier—usually not including uniform and weapons.

blockade

A barrier to stop people or supplies from entering a country or a port.

common green

A grassy area or park in the center of a town that can be used by everyone.

compulsory

Required or obligatory.

cutlass

A heavy sword with a curved blade commonly used by sailors and pirates.

de facto

Being in effect although not formally recognized.

dominant

Most in control; the most powerful.

encroachment

Exceeding intended limits, as of territory or property.

epidemic

An illness affecting a disproportionately large number of people in population or a region at one time.

execrable

Extremely inferior; very bad.

extirpate

To get rid of completely; to pull up by the root.

facings

A lining at the edge—especially of a garment.

forthwith

Without hesitation or delay.

freemen

Someone having the full rights of a citizen.

garrison

A military force located in a fort, village, or similar place.

homestead

A home and adjoining land occupied by a family.

impolitic

The show of bad judgment; unwise.

intelligence

Information gathered about an enemy, a possible enemy, or an area.

militia

A military force raised from the civilian population to supplement a regular army in an emergency.

moccasin

A soft leather heelless shoe or boot with the sole brought up the sides of the foot and over the toes

monopoly

Complete control of the entire supply of goods or of a service in a certain area or market.

pacifists

Those who oppose war and refuse to practice or acknowledge violence as a way of settling disputes.

piecemeal

Adding or doing one piece at a time.

privateers

Commanders or crew members on an armed ship commissioned by the state to capture or attack enemy ships in wartime.

provisions

The act of preparing and planning ahead for future needs; a supply of food and other necessary items.

public house

A facility that can be used by the populace; usually a tavern or an inn that has inexpensive accommodations.

Puritans

English Protestants of the sixteenth and seventeenth centuries, who sought to simplify the forms of worship in the Reformed Church of England.

reimburse

To pay someone an amount of money equal to the amount that was spent.

retaliation

Striking back; taking revenge.

ruthless

Having no mercy or sympathy; exhibiting cruelty.

Sabbath

The seventh day of the week, which is observed by most Christians as a day of rest and worship.

schooner

A ship that has at least two masts with the larger mast located toward the center and the shorter mast toward the front.

skirmish

A brief and often unplanned fight, especially between small or outlying parts of armies or fleets.

stealth

A secret, quiet, and clever way of moving or behaving.

stockades

A defensive enclosure or pen made with posts and stakes.

volley

A large number of bullets or arrows that are shot at the same time.

West Indies

The islands enclosing the Caribbean Sea; among them are Cuba, Hispaniola (Haiti and the Dominican Republic), Jamaica, and Puerto Rico.

Further Reading

Books

Anderson, Fred. *The War That Made America: A Short History of the French and Indian War*. New York, NY: Viking, 2005.

Chartrand, Rene. *Colonial Troops 1610 –1774*. Vols. 1–3. Oxford, UK: Osprey Publishing, 2002.

Chartrand, Rene. *American War of Independence Commanders (Elite)*. Oxford, UK: Osprey Publishing, 2003.

Martin, Joseph Plumb. *A Narrative of a Revolutionary Soldier: Some Adventures, Dangers, and Sufferings of Joseph Plumb Martin*. New York, NY: Penguin, 2010.

Walker, Sally M. *Written in Bone: Buried Lives of Jamestown and Colonial Maryland*. Minneapolis, MN: Carolrhoda Books, 2009.

Websites

Library of Congress

americaslibrary.gov/jb/colonial/jb_colonial_subj.html

Visit this Library of Congress website and discover what Abraham Lincoln had in his pockets on the night he was assassinated; find the settlers who landed on Plymouth Rock; learn about Buffalo Bill Cody and his "Wild West" show and the heroism of Harriet Tubman, who helped many slaves escape bondage.

Library of Congress, American Memory

memory.loc.gov/ammem/index.html

Explore the collections of the Library of Congress and other institutions through written and spoken words, sound recordings, still and moving images, prints, maps, and sheet music that document the American experience.

National Park Service

nps.gov/history/history/online_books/colonials-patriots/intro.htm

Experience American history through its more than 400 national parks, National Heritage Areas, and historic trails and waterways. Visit ancient archeological sites, read the stories that make up the country's shared history, and learn about the efforts to protect and preserve historical landmarks.

Road to Revolution

historyisfun.org/pdf/tea-overboard/RoadtoRevolution.pdf

Learn more about the "road to revolution," from the first landing at Jamestown to the beginning of the Revolutionary War. Read some of the arguments between the colonies and the British, and find out what King George III and Abigail Adams had to say.

Bibliography

Anderson, Fred. *Crucible of War: The Seven Years' War and the Fate of Empire in British North America, 1754–1766*. New York, NY: Random House, 2000.

Anderson, Fred. *The War That Made America: A Short History of the French and Indian War*. New York:, NY Viking, 2005.

Black, Col. Robert W. *Ranger Dawn: The American Ranger from the Colonial Era To the Mexican War*. Mechanicsburg, PA: Stackpole Books, 2009.

Chartrand, Rene. *Colonial American Troops 1610–1774*. Oxford, UK: Osprey Publishing, 2002.

Galvin, John R. *The Minutemen: A Compact History of the Defenders of the American Colonies 1645–1775*. New York, NY: Hawthorne Books, 1967.

Langguth, A.J. *Patriots: The Men Who Started the American Revolution*. New York, NY: Simon and Schuster, 1988.

Millett, Allan R., Peter Maslowski, and William B. Feis. *For the Common Defense: A Military History of the United States from 1607 to 2012*. New York, NY: Free Press, 2012.

Ross, John F. *War on the Run: The Epic Story of Robert Rogers and the Conquest of America's First Frontier*. New York, NY: Bantam Books, 2009.

Sanford, Elias Benjamin. *A History of Connecticut*. Boston, MA: Rand Avery, 1887.

Quotation Sources

Chapter One: Need for Defense

p. 6, Dalessandro, Colonel Robert, "Army Strong – Celebrating 400 Years of Service," www.army.mil/article/2695.

p. 7, Tyler, Lyon Gardiner. *Narratives of Early Virginia*, 1606–1625 (New York: Charles Scribner's Sons, 1907; reprinted New York, Barnes & Noble, 1959), p. 273.

p. 8, Lincoln, Charles Zebina, William H. Johnson, and Ansel Judd Northrup. *The Colonial Laws of New York* (Albany: New York State, 1894), p. 49.

p. 8, Jamestown Rediscovery, "James Fort," www.apva.org/rediscovery/page.php?page_id=383.

p. 8, Constitution Society, "Citizen Soldier," www.constitution.org/jw/acm_1-m.htm.

Chapter Two: Special Forces

p. 17, Rogers' Rangers, "Rules of Ranging, A 'Plan of Discipline' Extracted from Journals of Major Robert Rogers," www.rogersrangers.org/rules.

p. 17, Rogers' Rangers, "Rules of Ranging."

p. 17, Rogers' Rangers, "Rules of Ranging."

p. 18, American Experience, "Patriots Day," www.pbs.org/wgbh/amex/patriotsday/peopleevents/p_minutemen.html.

p. 19, Galvin, John R., *The Minutemen: A Compact History of the Defenders of the American Colonies 1645–1775* (New York: Hawthorne Books, 1967), p. 70.

Chapter Three: Early Battles

p. 22, Library of Congress, "Colonial Settlement, 1600s, Virginia's Early Relations With Native Americans," www.loc.gov/teachers/classroom-materials/presentationsandactivities/presentations/timeline/colonial/indians.

p. 24, Mashantucket Pequot Museum, "The History of the Pequot War," pequotwar.org/about.

p. 24, The Mashantucket (Western) Pequot Tribal Nation, "The Pequot War," www.mashantucket.com/pequotwar.aspx.

p. 25, Mystic Voices, "The Story of the Pequot War," www.pequotwar.com/history.html.

Chapter Four: Global Wars Go Local

p. 34, Stewart, Richard W. ed., "The United States Army and the Forging of a Nation, 1775—1917," www.history.army.mil/books/AMH-V1/ch02.htm.

p. 36, Henderson, Robert, ed., "A Soldier's Account of the Campaign on Quebec, 1759," www.militaryheritage.com/quebec1.htm.

p. 36, Henderson, "A Soldier's Account of the Campaign on Quebec, 1759."

Chapter Five: Celebration and Rebellion

p. 39, National Humanities Center, "Colonists Respond to British Victory in the French and Indian War, 1763," nationalhumanitiescenter.org/pds/makingrev/crisis/text1/britainvictorious1763.pdf.

p. 41, Anderson, Fred. *The War That Made America: A Short History of the French and Indian War* (New York: Viking, 2005), p. 233.

p. 42, Smith, Horace Wemyss. Life and Correspondence of the Rev. William Smith, D.D. (Charleston: Nabu Press, 2012), p. 371.

p. 42, Amherst College Library, "FAQs," amherst.edu/library/archives/faq.

p. 43, Anderson, *The War That Made America: A Short History of the French and Indian War*, p. 240.

Chapter Six: A New Battle, A New Army

p. 52, Massachusetts Historical Society, "Henry Knox Diary, 20 November 1775–13 January 1776," www.masshist.org/database/463/project15.

p. 52, New York State History Project, "The Knox Trail," www.nysm.nysed.gov/services/KnoxTrail/kthistory.html.

p. 54, Naval History and Heritage, "The Birth of the Navy of the United States," www.history.navy.mil/faqs/faq31-1.htm.

p. 55, Sons of the Revolution in the State of California, "Uniforms of the American Revolution," www.srcalifornia.com/uniforms/uniforms.htm.

Chapter Seven: Continental Army at War

p. 58, Library of Congress, "Creating a Continental Army," www.loc.gov/teachers/classroommaterials/presentationsandactivities/presentations/timeline/amrev/contarmy.

p. 61, Patterson, Benton Rain. *Washington and Cornwallis, the Battle for America, 1775–1783* (Boulder, CO: Taylor Trade and Publishing, 2004), p. 142.

p. 63, American Revolution Organization, "Letters from Valley Forge," www.americanrevolution.org/vlyfrgeltrs.html.

p. 63, Historic Valley Forge, "Who Served Here? Baron von Steuben," www.ushistory.org/valleyforge/served/steuben.html.

p. 64, Geist, Christopher, "A Common American Soldier," www.history.org/Foundation/journal/Autumn04/soldier.cfm.

p. 64, National Humanities Center, "Gen. George Washington Circular Letter of Farewell," nationalhumanitiescenter.org/pds/makingrev/independence/text1/washingtoncircularstates.pdf.

Index

Page numbers in **boldface** are images.

Author Biography

Carol Ellis has written many fiction and nonfiction books as well as classroom educational materials such as reading comprehension workbooks for younger students. Topics have included the history of Ancient Greece, the Gilded Age, African American activists and artists, and the development of hip-hop and rap.

Her research into the military of Colonial America provided an in-depth look at a fascinating, complex subject.

Ellis and her family live in New York and share their home with two cats.